Driving Sales
RESULTS

Driving Sales
RESULTS

The Startup Guide
to Successful Selling

Wolf Depauli

Contents

Starting up

Everyone sells every day. It's something most of us do without even thinking about it. Whether we're trying to convince our family of the merits of a hiking trip, or the best Friday night movie to attend, or if we're persuading a business colleague to agree to our latest and greatest idea — it's all about sales.

Bestselling author Daniel H. Pink wrote his book about selling, *To Sell Is Human: The Surprising Truth about Moving Others* (2012), after analysing his calendar entries and discovering: 'The picture that stared back was a surprise: I'm a salesman.'

I had a similar light bulb moment.

I used to sit on the other side of the fence. In my pre-sales life, I was a buyer for a large supermarket chain. My total buying volume was just under £140 million. At the time, I believed that most decisions, and certainly the best decisions, were based on a thoughtful analysis of the facts and figures. I believed that no sales professional could sell me anything unless it made factual sense for me to buy. That was until I met Walter.

It was hard not to like Walter. He was very passionate about his products and always found an opportunity to promote them, either directly or indirectly. He'd either manage to get me on the phone for a few minutes or drop me an email, or he would just happen to be near our offices and ask for a quick catch-up. All of these tactics could have gone terribly wrong if he hadn't executed them with style and thoughtfulness.

Walter had found a way to be persistent without being annoying or becoming a time-waster. He constantly asked questions and ran new ideas past me and the more he knew about our business the better his proposals became. But most importantly, the more we sold. I sold more to my customers and he sold more to me. Of course, not every idea was a golden, but he was clearly a guy who worked very hard to succeed and most of the time succeed he did.

After a few months we looked at the growth rate of his company and discovered that he had grown 10 times faster than his closest competitor. His products were good, but not 10 times better to justify the huge difference in growth rate. Ultimately, the success of his company was entirely down to him. Then it dawned on me that my 'just show me the facts' approach had gone out of the window. I was so intrigued by what Walter had accomplished that I decided to work in sales myself. And I'm glad that I did.

When I started in sales I was eager to learn all about the process, but I was disappointed by the lack and quality of literature on the subject that was available, so I began my own research with the goal of becoming a superior sales professional. I read academic papers, books, blogs, and magazines. I listened to podcasts and went to conferences. I learned from colleagues and friends, but most importantly, I learned on the job. Over many years I've collected a wealth of information which I've brought together in this book. It's structured so that you can easily and readily apply it to your personal environment.

3 is the Key

My most fundamental finding was that there are three key areas that form the foundation for sales success:

1. Method
2. Skills
3. Attitude

Method

This means having a plan and a process for how you undertake your sales activities. It's having clarity about who your target customers are, how you contact them, how many contacts you need, and how many deals you can expect to close in order to achieve your sales targets. This involves some record keeping, normally done with a Customer Relationship Management (CRM) tool like Salesforce, plus a little bit of analysis.

Skills

The second area is sales skills. Communication and commercial skills are at the heart of it. How do you write an email so that you get a response? How do you plan a presentation so that you get a yes at the end of the meeting? How do you structure the financials of an offer so that it works for your customer as well as for you? How do you deal with a stakeholder who is seemingly only interested in torpedoing your proposal?

Attitude

Arguably, attitude is important in every job, but as you will read later, attitude, and especially great attitude, sells. The very nature of sales means that rejection is part and parcel of the job. Managing your attitude is therefore a critical element of sales as it can make the difference between success and failure.

Whilst all three of these key areas are obviously important, they're pretty worthless in isolation. Being very skilled in sales, but following the wrong strategy means you're probably very good with customers, but not very effective in closing deals. Having a great strategy, but no skill to execute the strategy will equally fail. And a pessimistic attitude will defeat the best strategy and skill-set.

All of the three aspects need to be integrated and that's what you will learn in this book. The first few chapters are mainly concerned with method. Sales skills and attitude are covered later.

Who is this book for?

This book is about business-to-business (B2B) sales and focuses on finding and closing new deals. Whilst most of the content is also useful for dealing with existing customers (for example, account management), the main intention is to help you develop *new* and *existing* business.

This book is written for small companies, start-ups, entrepreneurs, individual sales professionals, freelancers and anyone who seeks to improve their sales approach and are willing to learn and implement new strategies. Some topics like sales skills, sales processes, analytics and attitude are universally applicable whether you work for a large or a small mature company or a start-up. That said, every sales professional has different circumstances, so all of the concepts discussed will require you to reflect on how they apply to your own specific situation. Let's get started.

CHAPTER 1

Where's the next deal please?

How you think about selling is crucially important for success. If you think of it as a testosterone-laden boxing match with your customer, every contact will look like a fight in the ring. Instead, think about sales as a 'one-to-one conversation with a potential buyer'. This conversation allows you to debate, ask questions, disagree, reflect and concur. Most importantly, it can be a fertile breeding ground for new ideas and solutions.

At heart, professional sellers and buyers are problem solvers who enjoy working on a challenge. They're the link to their businesses and both want to generate more value for their respective organisations. Try and remember this without any irony, if you can, the next time you sit opposite a buyer who wants to squeeze out every penny he can from your offer.

Whilst technology is changing our workplace and the way we communicate, the power of a conversation is unmatched. The more complex the service or product that is being sold, the greater the importance of intelligent interactions between smart sellers and smart buyers. Transactional sales jobs (travel agencies are a good example) have been under pressure due to the rise of the internet, but that's not a new phenomenon. Technological advances have *created* and *killed* jobs for decades. I'd argue, in fact, that for the growing number of knowledge workers in developed markets, selling, as part of their livelihood, has become more important than ever.

It's also important to note that a growing number of people today earn their living outside of the traditional model of being a permanent employee for a company. For them, work is not delivered and defined; instead, they have to create and find work themselves. In the UK in 2014 there were 4.6 million self-employed people — an increase of 732,000 since 2008 (Office for National Statistics, 2014). A few examples include: web designers, architects, photographers, consultants, event organisers, project managers and builders.

Unfortunately, many self-employed people are ill-prepared for the world of sales. That's hardly surprising since sales forms no part of the curriculum in schools or universities and that may well be why so many individuals have a problematic relationship with selling. That said, when I speak to small companies, sales is almost always one of their prime concerns. How do they make more sales? How do they create more predictable revenue streams? You'll discover the answers in the following pages.

Where's the line between marketing and sales?

But first let's address a common concern, and that's the line between marketing and sales. Particularly for small organisations that line is often blurred. If you're using social media to promote your product (and yourself) is that marketing or is that sales? What about organising a trade show? Marketing or sales? Does it matter?

For most small B2B companies, the lifeblood of the company is direct sales as the primary goal is to get new deals and to retain existing customers. So they don't have a separate marketing department.

That's understandable. There are two reasons for small companies to focus on sales and not on marketing. First, it's a matter of financial resources. Most small companies simply can't afford an additional person responsible for marketing. Second, some core marketing activities may not be practical and suitable for very small organisations e.g. market segmentation, product management, product positioning, and so forth.

Even when it's time for small companies to hire their first marketing head, it often has to be in a sales support role, focusing on the following activities:

- Developing collateral material for sales presentations and follow-ups
- Organising trade shows and events
- Managing the website and ensuring it is customer friendly
- Deploying marketing campaigns (on- and offline) to generate leads

It is only when companies grow and become more sophisticated that they recognise the need for a more professional marketing strategy. Marketing then becomes a department in its own right with specialist team members.

In B2B companies the marketing department is also mostly in charge of developing leads for sales. This means generating contacts and inbound leads of prospects.

The mere existence of you and your company and the services or products you offer will probably get you some enquiries. Increasing awareness of your company and its abilities is one of the activities for marketing. In practical terms that covers everything from attending trade shows and conferences, to organising sponsorships and, online advertising (Google, LinkedIn, Display advertising, etc.), and on to writing magazine articles, blogs, and white papers.

Provided these activities are executed well, they should result in customers coming to *you* instead of you having to find them. The internet has given marketing a boost in as much as the channels have become more transparent, especially for the marketer. You can assess with a good measure of accuracy how much business a Google AdWords campaign has delivered for you. You can also track the journey of your prospects and retarget them at other online locations (for example, serve them a display ad on a different website after they've left your site). In a world where most buyers extensively research potential purchases online before they make a decision, how you present yourself is crucially important.

To achieve the best results normally requires some alignment between sales and marketing. Common areas of conflict are sales departments accusing marketing of not producing enough or the right quality of inbound leads. Collecting business cards at trade shows for a chance of winning a prize might produce contact details, but not necessarily useful leads.

On the marketing side, a common issue with sales is the lack of quality and speed of engagement with new leads.

In my experience, however, both sides know the other field well. The methods of driving revenues might be different with marketing often going through indirect routes (think online advertising) and sales directly dealing with the customer (think sales meeting), but most sales professionals have a solid understanding of marketing strategies and vice versa.

But before we move on to the next chapter let me reiterate and expand a little on the three key areas I mentioned in the Introduction: 1. Method; 2. Skills; 3. Attitude.

Method

Method defines how you go about your sales activities. How do you proceed from having no customers and no contacts to closing a deal? What are the necessary steps to move from one stage to the next and how do you build a predictable sales pipeline? Method is about applying a structured approach to sales, so instead of just randomly looking for business, you define and follow a process to find, target and close customers.

The importance of a structured approach is often underestimated by most small companies. For example, you can randomly call contacts in the hope of getting business or you can segment your market by industry, size and location. If you knew that for every 15 calls to restaurants, you could close one deal, you already have a blueprint for your sales process. 10 deals needed? Call 150 restaurants. It is that simple — if you know your target customer and if you have a tried and tested method.

Skills

Skills refers to your personal ability to sell. For example, can you conduct a cold call? How do you respond to a request for tender? How do you negotiate a legal contract? How do you prepare a pitch? How do you handle objections in meetings? How good is your knowledge in your industry? Are you an expert in your industry?

I've met many sales professionals in my career, but I've yet to meet the best seller. I have met sales professionals however who have stopped learning and improving and as a result, so have their careers.

Attitude

Attitude is how you feel about yourself and others in your sales job. Regard it as your mental setup. How do you handle rejection? How do you prepare for a customer meeting? What is your attitude before making a cold call or before a meeting?

Attitude determines how you think about sales which in turn, will impact your results. This isn't just some motivational rah-rah advice — it's scientifically proven. Optimists sell. Pessimists fail. If you're pessimistic, grumpy and negative, your chances of being successful in sales is very limited.

Being successful in sales starts with knowing your product and your market. It starts with analysis and strategic thinking. These are all subjects I cover in the next chapter.

CHAPTER 2

Preparation

It begins in the boiler room. That's where the most successful sales professionals I have seen in the course of my career work hard to make the sale happen. You don't rush blindly into the market and pitch your products or services without preparation — unless you want to fail.

This chapter focuses on the need for *clarity*. It's about the need to fully understand your market, what it means for you and your customers.

The consequence of getting the basics wrong is costly. For example, if you've picked the wrong market and targeted the wrong leads your chances of success are greatly diminished. Perhaps with fatal consequences. Sometimes it takes trial and error to find out what works and what doesn't work. Actively selling and getting feedback is one of the best ways to learn about the market.

I know from experience how painful it is to venture into the market with a flawed product and a flawed strategy; when what looked good on a whiteboard or in a Word document doesn't survive the first real world customer contact.

At one point I was part of a team trying to sell a software-as-a-service solution. It had some nice features but frankly it was immature for the market and inferior to competitive products. I was working for a well-known brand so that certainly helped us to get conversations with potential customers and we even managed to sign a few deals. But the product and the distribution strategy was just a mess.

Nevertheless, we kept dialling away. But the company (and the sales force) would have been better advised to reset and take a good, hard look at a strategy that wasn't succeeding. It became obvious to me that the product had no future so I left the company. Today the company has pulled the product from most markets and in the one country where it's still sold, it's been scaled down to a fraction of what it once was. In all fairness, the bad sales strategy was just an extension of a bad marketing and product strategy, but executing a bad strategy means you're spinning your wheels.

Before reaching out to customers, I prepare my key questions carefully:

- What problem am I solving for my customer?
- Why would somebody buy from me?
- Who is my customer?
- How do I sell profitably?

You must do this for every customer. Markets, products, competitors and technologies continually evolve requiring you to challenge your preconceptions regularly. With greater clarity, the easier you'll make a sale.

Driving Sales Results

What problem are you solving for your customer?

Why does your customer need you? *What does your product mean to your customer?* Viewed from a slightly different angle you could ask: *How do I want my customer to perceive my product?* What does it do for them? Harvard Business School professor Theodore Levitt is famous for saying, 'People don't want to buy a quarter-inch drill. They want a quarter-inch hole!' Imagine that you're handed a drill and simply told, 'Sell it'. You might be tempted to get into a detailed description about all of the fine features of the drill and the manufacturing process and so forth, but what really matters to the buyer is that they need the drill for a project. They need to drill a hole. So whatever you sell, just make sure you're not confusing the product (the drill) with the solution for the customer (the hole).

In order to get clarity about your own offering, analyse it in the context of your customer base and look at their buying behaviour. Why did they buy? What problem did your product solve for them?

Here's an example. I sold a mobile app solution to help app developers make extra revenues by adding a storefront to their app. This revenue is potentially significant to small start-ups as every penny counts when you first start your business.

However, the storefront extension is also relevant to larger companies. It makes their app more relevant and interesting to their users. While I use the money argument when talking to small app developers, I avoid it when speaking to larger companies. Incremental revenues of £20,000 a month might be great for a small start-up, but it's not a sum that gets a corporate executive out of bed. Execs want to know how this extension can make their app more interesting and how it would increase user engagement rates.

If you need more insights about your new customer base, conduct a little market research by reaching out to businesses and asking them about their issues and buying behaviours relating to your product. I've always found that when you ask for feedback most people are happy to give it to you. It's also a very inexpensive exercise. All it needs is a little effort on your part. It's not a scientific survey. The results are anecdotal, but valuable nevertheless.

Why would somebody buy from you?

Of course, you could be the greatest sales professional in the world and there might still be some excellent reasons why customers won't buy from you. Unless you're in a unique market position i.e. you have a monopoly; customers will always have choices. That means, that if they don't like yours they can simply go somewhere else to buy a similar product. What's even worse is if they didn't buy from you in the first place because they couldn't figure out what your product represents.

Product positioning isn't just a sales responsibility but if you want to succeed in sales you have to own it. And note that you can't be everything to everyone. Ultimately your company's strategy (or, if you're a freelancer, your individual positioning) will dictate your sales approach. While there are subtle nuances to each, there are three basic choices. You can either 1) compete on cost/price; 2) offer something different; or 3) be a niche player. Does that sound like a lofty strategic discussion that shouldn't apply to sales? Well, I know several sales professionals who struggle because they have not clarified their position in the market. This 'choice' or lack thereof, trickles very quickly down to your sales pitch.

For example, for on cost or price leadership, your sales message could evolve around: 'I won't be beaten on price'. In this case, you're hopefully not only offering the lowest price, you (ideally) also have the lowest cost-structure. Otherwise, your model may not be sustainable.

For differentiation, the message be, 'You can't find this solution anywhere else'.

Differentiation is also 'delivered' in the sales process. If you understand your customer better, make a better offer, bring a better solution and so on, the entire differentiation can come from sales.

The niche player understands a small subset of the market extremely well and the contextual sales message would be, 'We are the experts in this industry'.

The danger is that if you don't fall into any of these categories you're stuck somewhere in the middle, where you can't effectively compete in any of the categories. Some companies are cheaper, some have more features, and others are experts in one specific area. This doesn't leave much oxygen for someone who is a 'Jack of all Trades'.

The relevancy for small companies

Now let's turn to some of the advantages of being a small company. First of all, small companies are better positioned to be able to get immediate feedback from the customer. They can be close to the client, in every sense of the word. If you lose deals because your pricing is too high or you're missing key features — you will hear the reason from your customers first hand. Where small companies often tend to struggle is the translation of 'what just happened with this customer' into a response or strategy that addresses the issue. For example, if you have a differentiated product, but you're trying to sell it to a price sensitive customer, you'll inevitably experience friction in sales. If you're selling a differentiated product, but your target customer doesn't appreciate or understand your key features, you need to work on your product offering. The problem smaller companies sometimes experience is that their 'can do' attitude means they try to be everything to everyone, which normally doesn't work.

Clarity on your positioning will make your life easier in sales. If you're offering a premium solution certain customer segments — i.e. those who are price sensitive — won't be a fit for you. So don't target them in the first place. Or if you happen to get into a situation where there's a mismatch (e.g. price war) you can excuse yourself from the discussion gracefully. Knowing where you stand in the market will allow you to pick your battles and use your time more effectively.

Below is a short case study describing the effects of a product-customer mismatch and the long-term effects on the sales professional.

....

Case Study: Customer Fit

George has been in the printing industry for many years and witnessed the transition from offset (analogue) printing to digital printing first hand. Digital printers are more flexible because they can print lower volumes cost effectively. Supposedly.

At the time, George was a strong supporter of the new digital printers because he, like so many, saw this as the future. George went out and started selling. The machines weren't cheap, but the market showed immediate interest and deals were coming through. The promise of more flexibility and better cost-control were killer arguments for prospects in a cut-throat market with fierce competition. Customers were receptive to any innovation that would give them an edge over the competition.

George continued to extoll their virtues to the market and making sales. However, a problem slowly arose. Since these digital printers were 'first generation' machines, they weren't as easy to use as promised. It took time and expertise to set up the machines for each single job so the hailed flexibility rarely materialised. Consequently, many of his customers switched back to their analogue printing machines. The tide had turned and customers were expressing their anger about the product. These were painful times for George, but eventually the digital machines improved and so did customer satisfaction.

George learned an important lesson from this experience. He makes sure that each prospect has a real use for their digital printers. If a client just wants to buy one because the technology looks appealing, he tends to talk them out of it. It sounds absurd, but George prefers to walk away from a deal than to close a bad one. He's in it for the long-term, hence he's not interested in dissatisfied clients. His credibility pays his salary so he doesn't mess with it.

Selling is about connecting companies and people, and if these connections lead to a bad deal, the relationship is tarnished. It may be acceptable for a sales professional who is 'just travelling through' until the next job comes along, but for those committed to building sustainable relationships that's not an option.

Who is your customer?

One of the main sales activities is to actively engage potential customers. In order to do that you need to know who you're supposed to engage with, who your target customer is and where you can find them. It could be as precise as 'companies with an annual budget between £100,000 and £1,000,000 who have outsourced call-centres and are at the end of their contract'. How could you possibly know who's looking for a new supplier amongst the thousands of companies engaged in providing customer services through call centres? The solution lies in segmenting to narrow down the market from 'everyone' to companies which are more likely to be within your target group.

The quality of this segmentation process has implications throughout the entire sales process. It's the basis for generating leads — the very leads you'd eventually hope to close as deals. It's easy to see how bad targeting and bad segmentation will affect your entire sales performance. The better you define your target, the more skilfully you segment your market, the higher the chances of closing deals.

Here are some popular segmentation options:

Revenue/business size

Most products are built and sold to certain sized companies. It makes a difference if your product is for enterprise customers (large) or SMB's (small and medium sized businesses). Some products are sold across the entire range of small to big companies. Microsoft Windows is a good example. But usually the company size will define your offering. Even if your product has wide applicability, chances are that you still have to adjust your sales approach depending on the company type. Large companies have multiple stakeholders and influencers, whilst in small companies it's still the owner who makes most decisions.

Industry

It's likely that you'll find a concentration of potential customers in certain industries. If you're selling software security solutions to the banking industry, then obviously banking is your target industry. On the other hand, catering services are almost industry agnostic. Caterers can operate a canteen in a school just as well as in a bank or a pharmaceutical company.

Segmenting your market into verticals (verticals is the term used to define industries or subcategories of that industry) has benefits beyond targeting. Gaining insights into an industry will make you an expert over time and you'll become better at selling to those customers. (See section: What problem are you solving for your customer?)

Geography

Residents of rural areas in Scotland buy winter tyres, but Londoners are less likely to do so. In the same way your distribution might face geographical limitations (think field sales). If your product can be sold over the phone or online, your reach will be wider than if you have to sell in person. Then there's also a language and cultural barrier. If you're unfamiliar with the market and don't speak the language, it's that much harder to start selling into a market.

Size of the deal

The bigger the deal, the more time you and your organisation can spend on it. The cost of travelling is offset by the potential reward if you close the deal. When is a deal big? It depends. Below is an example of how you can calculate the financial viability of physically visiting customers.

Cost per visit (labour and expenses) £250

Average number of visits per potential customer 2

Close rate of all potential customers visited 30%

Margin per deal (sale per deal minus variable
(product) costs) £2,000

Table 1 shows the calculated profitability of your customer visits.

2,000 × 30%	Margin per deal, multiplied by close rate (30%)
= 600	Average expected profit for one customer visit
− 500	Average cost for one customer visit
= 100	**Contribution margin to cover your fixed costs**

Table 1: Profitability of customer visits

In this case it would be profitable for you to continue making those customer meetings. It's arguably a simplified model, but it's a method to understand the financial implications of going to a meeting. There's no hard and fast rule for how to handle this. If you're just starting off in sales you may want to grab every opportunity to be in front of customers — and that's probably the right thing to do. Being overly conscious about the cost-per-visit impact at this stage could be detrimental to the ramp-up phase most companies are going through. In these situations you want to use as many opportunities as possible to be in front of a customer.

Segmentation is important to make sure you're working on the right customer segment. As discussed, classic segmentation criteria are revenue/business size, industry, geography and size of deal. With these criteria you can then build your own leads list (more detail to come on this topic).

How do you sell profitably?

'Revenue is vanity, profit is sanity' as the saying goes. Selling profitably, in its simplest form, is having money left once all the costs have been paid. It's equally important to collect the money from your customer once you've closed the deal, especially when you are a small company. To make sure you receive the money you're owed, you can put precautions in place. For instance, always check the credit rating of your potential customer and have credit insurance in place which covers you for any potential loss. Getting paid can be a real challenge in certain industries and, in general, companies don't fold because they're unprofitable, but because they run out of cash. You can run a profitable business, but still go bust if you can't maintain a positive cash-flow.

Pricing and price-negotiations are, of course, classic sales topics. Many books have offered extensive advice on the subject of how you should handle pricing objections. It's deemed to be one of the most common objections and so you need to have a strategy to deal with it. You, as the sales professional, will want to generate the highest profit achievable, but likewise your buyer will strive to accomplish the opposite – the lowest price possible. Here, I'm going to concentrate on pricing.

Finance looks at pricing by distinguishing two cost blocks: *variable* costs (what it actually costs to make the product) and *fixed* costs (rent, staff, insurance, etc.). Fixed costs are independent of you selling a single product because you'll still have to pay the rent regardless of how well your business does.

The reason I mention fixed and variable costs here is because in practice it is not always as straightforward as it seems. The fixed cost allocation can create problems when product prices vary. For example, if you're selling a £300 product alongside a £5 product and you simply divide your fixed cost by the total number of units sold, both products would be 'loaded' with the same amount. Let's assume you sold 1,000 units and your fixed costs are £15,000 so each unit would get a fixed cost allocation of £15 (15,000 / 1,000). That's a mere 5 percent extra for the £300 (£315) item, but it's a 400 percent increase for the £5 (£20) item. In this case, a weighted allocation might be a better alternative where you mark up each item by a certain percentage (e.g. 20%).

It doesn't stop there as budgets and prices are built on assumptions of how many units you'll sell in the next year. If that assumption is wrong, so is your product calculation.

In table 2, the forecast was to sell 40 units so the fixed cost per unit sold would be £2,500 and the variable costs £500. If the actual number sold is only 25, the fixed cost per unit would raise to £4,000. It also works the other way round: if you sold 60 units, the fixed cost per unit goes down to £1,667.

If you had gone out to the market with a customer price of £4,000 you'd either be desperate in scenario 1 (cost per unit increases by +34%) or delighted in scenario 2 (cost per unit goes down by -39%). It goes to show that a few units up or down can make all the difference and it's yet another reason to make sure that your sales are predictable.

	Forecast	Revised Scenario	Revised Scenario
Variable cost per unit	500	500	500
Fixed cost	100,000	100,000	100,000
Units sold	50	35	65
Fixed cost per unit	2,000	2,857	1,538
Total cost per unit	2,500	3,357	2,038
Change to total cost		+34%	-39%

Table 2: Forecasting costs

For practical reasons many organisations work to target margins, which is the percentage difference between the sales price and the variable product cost. In the example above, if the sales price was £4,000 and the variable costs were £500 that margin would be

£3,500. In percentages it would be 88 percent (3,500 divided by 4,000). The margin is then used to cover the fixed costs, in this case £2,500, and to hopefully earn a profit. Arguably, the fixed costs in this example are rather high, but that's not uncommon for small companies — agencies, for example. For agencies most of the costs are salaries, rent and utilities which are all fixed. These businesses have hardly any variable costs as all the costs are tied up in running the service in the first place.

I once worked in a company where I was in charge of the export business, and our competitive pricing was crucial to secure deals. The finance team would give me a price range I could charge, and they also set up an export profit and loss statement so we could monitor the performance independent of the rest of the business.

At some point, we went through the export cost structure line by line. Amongst other things I discovered the export business was charged a percentage of the field-sales cost, despite the fact that no field-sales team had ever set foot onto export markets. The allocation was almost £50,000 and made a real difference to our profitability.

Pricing models

In recent years, there's been a silent revolution around new and innovative pricing models. Consider the Internet and its free services paid by advertising (e.g. Google Maps) or low-cost airlines, which have found innovative ways to deconstruct airfares (e.g. EasyJet). In both cases it's backed up by a great business model, but nevertheless attractive pricing is a major part of their success.

Below is a list of the most common pricing models.

- **Cost model**
  The total cost of making the product is the basis for setting the price at a defined margin.

- **Value model**
  Setting the price at the perceived value for the customer —
  in other words, the maximum price the customer is
  willing to pay. Example: many theme parks sell photo
  prints and photo merchandise. These products cost a few
  pence to print, but they are sold at an absolute premium
  (£20 or more) because they have a high emotional value
  to the visitor who, in that specific situation, is willing
  to pay the price.

- **Portfolio pricing**
  This is a very common practice in supermarkets as they
  usually stock thousands of products. They often use low
  priced anchor items to get the customer into the shop.
  Some might even be sold at a loss (if legally permitted).
  This loss is normally offset by other, higher margin products in the customer's basket so that overall the supermarket turns a profit.

- **Tiered pricing**
  For example, one treatment costs £10, five cost £40 and 10
  cost £80.

- **Competitive pricing**
  The competition is the benchmark for setting the price.

- **Feature pricing**
  Entry price for a no-frills version of the product and any
  additional features are charged extra. (Think about how
  different types of cars are sold).

- **Captive pricing model**
  Also known as the razor-blade model. The razor itself is
  sold at a very low price, but the blades come at a premium.
  This pricing is also popular with printers and cartridges.
  The idea is to lock the customer into a system so that they
  need to 'refill' consumables at premium prices.

- **Pricing models in the online world**
  - **Free**
    The product (or service) is completely free and the business is financed by advertising (e.g. Gmail, Facebook).

  - **Free with paid support**
    The product is free, but service and support are sold for a fee (e.g. Magento, an e-commerce platform which is free, but any support or service needs to be paid for).

  - **Freemium**
    The basic version of the product is free, but a better version has to be paid for (e.g. Spotify).

  - **Paid**
    Surprisingly, some companies still charge you for their services.

How decisive pricing can be is well illustrated by Xerox's launch of photocopiers back in the 1960s. It was a revolutionary product at the time and Xerox struggled with a slow take-up due to the high price point of the copy-machines. The company decided to change its pricing policy to a pay-per-copy model and the business thrived. This pricing model gave customers the opportunity to test the new technology without making a huge upfront commitment and once customers experienced the advantages first hand, they really took to it.

Conclusions

All of this preparation work has one goal, namely to make the selling process easier. It's a little like keeping your house in order. Knowing how you can help customers, knowing why they should buy from you, knowing who it is you should speak to, and knowing how to make money with your business are fundamental sales questions must be answered. Clarity is bliss.

The next step is to translate these strategic considerations into practical, actionable activities like lead generation which is the subject of the next chapter.

CHAPTER 3

Getting started with leads

When I speak to small companies where the managing director also involuntarily acts as the sales director, I almost always observe a lack of a structured sales approach or method.

These companies often have good intentions. They are certainly not short on ambition. And, in general, they have an instinct for closing deals. But selling activities are often conducted at random. Sales only becomes a priority when there's spare time or when there's an apparent lack of new revenues. The absence of a method manifests itself in different ways, but one of the fundamental and most pressing issues is not processing enough leads each week, month, quarter, and year.

Working with leads is a little bit like farming. You need to plough the field and then sow the crop before you can harvest. Your sales pipeline works in a very similar fashion, but if you want to harvest all year round you can never stop generating and qualifying leads. It really has to be a continuous process. Without leads there are no opportunities and without opportunities there are no deals. The only way to achieve this is by working methodically — understanding that sales is a system where each stage needs constant attention and where each stage can't function without the other.

Sales method

Working methodically means *breaking sales down into separate stages* so each can be managed and evaluated separately. Generating and qualifying leads, working on opportunities and closing deals is then no longer muddled up in an undefined process.

As part of the process you *measure* each stage, you collect data about your activities, you *analyse* and *iterate* on the basis of your findings. Consequently, performance *evaluation* becomes more qualitative as it moves away from a generic 'we're not getting enough sales' to addressing specific issues like 'we're processing 50 leads a month, but our lead-to-opportunity-rate has fallen to 20 percent'. The latter understanding allows you to investigate and fix a defined issue and introduces a level of *accountability* with fewer wishy-washy performance explanations such as 'tough market', 'fierce competition' and 'difficult customers'.

As a general rule of thumb, the larger the company the more specialised the sales organisation becomes with individual teams looking after lead generation, lead qualification, selling, sales operations, account management for exiting clients and so on.

Smaller companies or individual sellers can't operate on that basis, but they can still work methodically. At the heart of the sales process is the infamous 'funnel' as shown in Figure 1. It's called a funnel, because opportunities flow through it with the highest volumes at the top and decreasing numbers as you move towards the bottom. It's easier to get conversations in the early stage, but harder to find businesses which ultimately buy from you.

Driving Sales Results

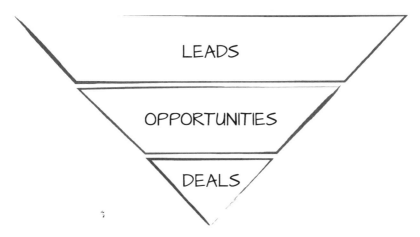

Figure 1: The sales funnel

Leads

Leads are contacts. If it's an outbound lead, you might have little more than a company name. If it's an inbound lead, you'd normally have the contact details and a description of the area of interest.

Opportunities

Opportunities are *qualified* leads. In other words you have an indication that this company might end up buying from you.

Deals

Deals don't require much explanation!

The often used phrase, 'Sales is a numbers game', describes the notion that you need to 'feed' your funnel with a sufficient number of leads to realistically achieve a certain (lower) number of deals. This lower success rate is a totally expected behaviour. If all of your leads turn into deals you have an unbelievable business on your hands and you should hire more sales professionals as quickly as you can.

Leads die fast for all sorts of reasons. In the first instance, when you try to qualify a lead, you may never manage to get through to the right contact or you may be told flat-out that there's just no interest in your product. You may be too late as the company's already signed with a competitor. You may be too expensive. The list of reasons for rejections can go on and on, but the fact remains that leads perish quickly so you need to maintain a steady stream of leads coming into the funnel.

Selling in general and lead qualification in particular is a bit like matchmaking. Sometimes you're not the right match for your prospect and sometimes the prospect is not the right fit for you. Selling is about finding out whether or not a business relationship can be established — and both parties have equal rights in this process; it's not just the buyer 'calling the shots', it's also the sales professional reserving the right to walk away from an unsuitable lead.

Defining leads

There are two types of leads: *warm* and *cold*. Cold leads are contacts you have never been in touch with before. For example, if you want to sell to Tesco, but you only have the company name on a leads list with no contact details, you have an extremely cold (arctic!) lead staring back at you.

In contrast, when a lead is warm, somebody has shown an interest in your product i.e. they contacted you. Warm leads typically come from sources like referrals, website forms, trade shows, etc.

Very close to the definition of warm and cold leads are 'inbound' and 'outbound' leads. Whilst warm and cold describe the *status* of the prospect, inbound and outbound describe the *method* of approach. In reality that equates to the same thing, meaning an *inbound* lead is *warm*: Somebody approaches you (inbound) wanting to buy (warm), as opposed to *you* contacting a target (outbound) to sell your product (cold).

In addition to warm and cold leads, there are 'qualified' and 'unqualified' leads. Leads are qualified when they've passed some established criteria which make them eligible for the sales pipeline as shown in Figure 2.

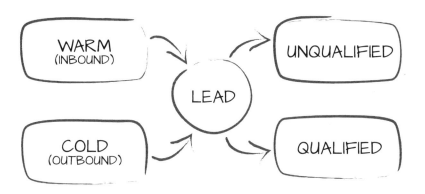

Figure 2: Lead flow

What truly makes a lead qualified? The most popular qualification concept is called BANT (Budget, Authority, Need, Time). This concept will be discussed in more detail later in this chapter, but in essence, if your leads don't tick all BANT boxes, they might not be of good enough quality for the pipeline and no lead should be put into the sales pipeline unless there's a realistic chance of it becoming a deal. The reasons for disqualifying a lead will vary and can range from 'not interested' (no need), 'too expensive' (no budget), 'too much effort to implement' (no time), to 'all buying decisions are made in Tokyo' (no authority).

It doesn't mean that you give up on a lead at the first point of resistance, but if there's a real issue you can't move the lead into the pipeline. Keep the lead on hold and revisit it at a later stage. Circumstances can change and a few quarters down the line the situation might be entirely different. BANT is a great framework, but it's not without its shortcomings.

This part of the book focuses on lead-qualification, but I'm keen to stress that it's equally important to excite your prospect in the process. In fact, creating attention and interest comes before any qualification, but eventually both processes have to go hand in hand. Composing this conversation is the art of sales. I'm deliberately using the word *composing* here, because it takes time, creativity, testing and work to get it right. More about this later in Chapter 6.

Some years ago, I was working on a deal with a large blue-chip retailer. They were interested in a bespoke product solution of ours, which had the potential of doing millions of pounds in revenues on their websites. Early on I sensed some concerning signals. First of all, they hinted at very aggressive purchasing conditions which would have left us with wafer-thin margins, something I'd have had a very hard time justifying (BANT: budget issue). Secondly, launching our product on their catalogue required them to do some work and it was unclear if they would ever complete this (BANT: time).

They invited us and a few other companies to pitch for the deal. We pitched hard, even though I was constantly in two minds whether we should proceed or not. However, the challenge following BANT under such circumstances was that *the prize was too big for us to walk away.*

Long story short, they didn't buy from us. But neither did they buy from any other supplier. The retailer never launched anything in this space. We had wasted time and money, but we would have kicked ourselves had we not engaged in the deal and a competitor had won it. The take-away from this story is that you often sense the problems early on and sometimes you just have to play along.

But if you have too many of these pie-in-the-sky type of opportunities your pipeline is as solid as a house of cards.

The first steps in generating leads is actually having absolute clarity about your target customer. For some businesses it can be crystal clear, while for others it can be quite a challenge. In a way it's as much about targeting companies as it is about saying no to others. Almost every company has a sweet spot of companies with which they'd like to work. A practical example would be a marketing agency for e-commerce (industry) with revenues of up to £100m (size) located in the UK (geography). Figure 3 shows lead definition criteria.

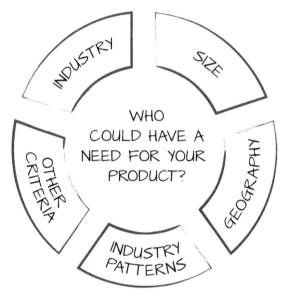

Figure 3: Lead definition

Why would you define leads anyway? If you're working in a digital agency turning its head to any project that's within the remits of its capabilities, you have to narrow down the target list in order to do any meaningful sales work. Once you have more clarity about your target, you can start generating leads. Small companies normally apply a DIY approach to building leads lists and collecting leads from various sources. Medium- and large-sized companies tend to have a lead generation system and use marketing automation to drive inbound leads.

Generating leads

You have two distinct ways to generate leads. The first is to start with a list of target customers and then contact them one by one (outbound leads).

The second is to drive inbound leads which is more of a marketing play due to its indirect nature. The obvious channels for inbound leads are online marketing, partnership deals or advertising (e.g. trade magazines).

Competing on search engines is nothing more than competing for customers who have already shown an interest in your product range. If somebody puts 'team training' into a search engine, at the very least they're actively looking for more information about the topic; at best they're seeking a company from which they can buy a team training product or service. If you provide team training and they click on your link, visit your website and request more information you have created an inbound lead. Due to the growing importance of the Internet and the changes in buying behaviour, the effort to drive inbound leads has increased substantially and a number of companies have sprung up to offer turnkey solutions in this field (e.g. Marketo, Hubspot, Salesforce).

There are different ways to generate inbound and outbound leads and Figure 4 below features the most prominent lead sources. The top 3 areas indicate sources for *outbound* leads and the bottom 3 areas show sources for *inbound* activities. *Referrals* don't really fit into either category; they fall in-between inbound and outbound leads.

> BUYING LISTS
  > BUILDING LISTS
    > EVENTS AND TRIGGER SITUATIONS
      > REFERRALS
        > PARTNERS
          > ONLINE LEAD GENERATION
            > CONTENT STRATEGY

Figure 4: Generating leads

Buying lists [outbound]

Buying or renting lists comes at a cost and you need to specify what exactly you are looking for — industry, geography, company size, etc. Dun & Bradstreet, Hoovers, Data.com (part of Salesforce) are well-known and reputable companies in this space, but there is a growing number of smaller agencies and individuals that now provide the same service.

When using a list to email a large audience you need to make sure the list owner has the permission of the people on the list. It is generally not permitted in the UK (and most other countries) to send unsolicited mass-emails unless the recipients have actively opted-in. The responsibility for this may lie with the list owner, but it will reflect badly on you and your company, and it could have legal consequences, if you receive a complaint from governing bodies such as the ASA (Advertising Standards Agency).

Also, be realistic about the performance of mass emails as conversion rates tend to be low. Even if people have consented to receive promotional emails, they haven't signed up to receive email from you, so you'll be hitting people who have no intention of ever buying from you.

List owners normally give you some reference conversion rates, but bear in mind that they want to sell their data so it's unlikely that they will share really bad performance figures with you. Forecast a realistic range of expected contacts (from pessimistic->realistic->optimistic) so that you're set up for the inbound leads you're generating. There is no point in sending emails if you don't have the capacity to follow up on enquiries.

Working with email lists and digital media requires an understanding of digital marketing in general. For example, designing emails, creating copy, tracking performance and offering prospects a consistent experience throughout your online touch points is a job in its own right. If you lack this expertise, you will need to find someone who has it; otherwise, it's unlikely that this is going to work for you.

Many sales teams refuse to work with bought lists at all as they're prone to contain errors and often require a lot of extra work.

If your inbox looks a bit like mine, you get unsolicited sales emails every day. I happen to be on one of the big data company's list who got everything wrong apart from my name and my email address, which means I get emails all the time from blue-chip companies trying to sell me products which are completely irrelevant to me. Most rented or bought lists will be used for emailing, but using them as a phone list is certainly an option (provided the list comes with phone numbers).

Working with third party lists can give your lead generation effort a boost, but it's hardly the silver bullet that many data companies want to make you believe it is.

Building lists [outbound]

Building your own list is the DIY option and, most likely, the most economical way to generate outbound leads. For small companies that don't have to constantly feed a big sales organisation with fresh leads, it's a very sensible and cost-effective approach.

How do you do it? Your lead definition (industry, geography, size, etc.) forms the segmentation criteria and then you simply start researching to build your list. Below are a few obvious places to go to:

Search engines

For example: You want to build a list of medium-sized camera retailers in the UK — online and offline.

Play with keywords on search engines (for example use the words 'camera' and 'shop') and go through the search-result pages to see if your query has produced anything of value. Note down each company until you reach a point where the results are no longer relevant. For each result, capture the company name, website and any contact details available. You can then try different keywords or iterations of keywords as this often generates new results (for example 'camera accessories'). By doing this, you should be able to develop a good base list for this segment.

I use search engines for all sorts of investigative jobs. Background on companies and people, and general market information. If you want company updates on a regular basis, you may want to look into aggregators like Feedly or Google Alerts that summarise the news and put them in one place.

Another way to use search engines is to look for contact details. Sometimes you can find the email address or a telephone number of a company or person on the web.

LinkedIn

LinkedIn has a few hundred million members worldwide and a significant number in the UK and Europe, although it's worth noting that in some European countries other platforms are popular too. For example, Xing.com in Germany or Viadeo.com in France.

I personally don't know any sales professional who isn't using LinkedIn in one way or another. With the popularity of LinkedIn have come paid products like Sales Navigator and Recruiter Lite. The functionality of the paid products has grown over time and so has the pricing. It's become quite expensive to buy an annual license (currently around £500+ per year for the Sales Navigator).

For starters, you need a profile and I assume most readers will have one. If you're operating across different European markets, you may also want to create a profile on the more regional platforms (e.g. Xing, Viadeo). Your profile should be up to date and free of spelling errors. My personal irritants are photos or the lack thereof on the profile page. Anyone with a cropped wedding photo where red-eyes have been retouched amateurishly looks unprofessional. Neither is LinkedIn the place to show off your family (posting baby photos is for Facebook). You can get an adequate portrait shot from £50 upwards and can use the same photo for a few years. If you break down the investment per year, it'll works out quite reasonable.

With regards to career history and profile information, most people, including myself, aren't interested in reading an essay so keep it short and simple.

Skills on LinkedIn are the one- or two-word phrases that are shown on your profile page, for example 'Business Development'. Having been endorsed for skills is good and gives the impression of an active profile. Getting endorsements often works on a reciprocal basis. If you endorse others, you're more likely to be endorsed in return. People sometimes need a little nudge. Ask friends, good colleagues and acquaintances for endorsements. They're normally willing to help.

I've personally not cared much about reviews (i.e. personal recommendations on your profile page) and my opinion it's more important for job-hunting than sales, but I could be convinced otherwise. I'm sure LinkedIn has a statistic somewhere that proves that x reviews increase your deal-close rate by y%.

Keep in mind that people listed on LinkedIn will have different motives to use the platform. Not everyone will take LinkedIn as seriously as sales professionals. Executives high up in the hierarchy may have a LinkedIn profile, but may not be very active. Some people won't have a profile at all. People in technical professions sometimes use LinkedIn for job-hunting, but are absent otherwise. Not everyone you see on LinkedIn is going to be an active user.

Is a free account sufficient for sales?

In my view, it depends on how you generate your leads. For example, I often start with a company target list that I've put together elsewhere. I go to LinkedIn, search for the company name to find out if they have a company page. If it's a strategic prospect, I might decide to follow the company (look for the 'Follow' button on the company page). Following a company will serve you company updates in your message board on LinkedIn.

On the same company page, you will find a link 'View All' which gives you the list view of all company employees. Once you're on the employee list page you can use 'Advanced Search' to filter down further. Keep in mind that the current free version only shows you full profiles up to third-degree connections.

Once, and if you've found the right contact, you have two options. You can connect with the person where you'll be asked to confirm how you know them. It is against LinkedIn's terms and conditions to connect with someone you don't know and LinkedIn have even gone as far as to put obstacles to discourage this. If you don't know a person, it is possible to choose one of the options shown in a drop-down menu like 'We have done business together' but please be aware you could fall foul of LinkedIn's anti-spam procedures.

The risk of this approach is that the recipient will see your invite alongside three options. 1) 'Accept', 2) 'I don't know *xyz*' or 3) 'Spam'. If the recipient declines and chooses option 2 or 3 and you had more than 5 of those, your account may be restricted and from there on out, you'll be required to put in the email address *every* time you want to connect with someone, even if you have a 'legitimate' history (e.g. colleague, done business together, etc.).

Alternatively, you can make an informed guess about the person's company email address. Most companies have an email convention that caries through the entire organisation. It could be:

[1st letter of the first name]+[surname]@[company].com.

So John Smith from Acme.com would be jsmith@acme.com. The email convention of the company is normally not too hard to find. Go to the company's press page (if they have one), some companies still have support email addresses (and not just web forms). There's also a more sophisticated way to do this by using an 'email permutator' in Excel or Google Sheets that allows you to create the most likely email addresses by providing 1) First Name, 2) Last Name and 3) the company domain. Once all options are calculated, you then copy them over to your email programme where you paste them into the send box. Before you do that, you need to enable the social plugin for your email program. Microsoft Outlook has its own, for Gmail I recommend Rapportive. Afterwards hover over each email address until you see the person's profile showing up on the social plugin. This works only if the email address has been used on social networks. Go to wolfonsales.com/emails for more information.

If you don't have any contact details you can ask a mutual connection to introduce you to the prospect (only for 2nd degree connections). On the member's profile page, click on the facing down arrow next to 'Send *xyz* InMail' and then click on the link 'Get introduced'.

You don't have to make contact in writing when you've found somebody on LinkedIn. You may just try to call the company.

By the way, whilst you're on a prospect's profile page, always look at the 'People also viewed' section on the right hand side. It might show you other potential leads.

Paid Version

The paid version, besides offering much more functionality, is great if your entry point isn't a company, but a persona search. Say for example you're looking for a 'VP of HR' in companies with more than 500 employees in London with the post-code W2. LinkedIn lets you add additional filters like relationship and seniority level. Unlike the free version, you'll be able to see pretty much anyone on LinkedIn who matches your criteria. You'd find it very hard in the free version to make the 'persona' search work.

You can also save results as leads directly in LinkedIn, get updates when anything changes and send 'InMail', contacting prospects directly without risk of penalty as in the free version. InMail is restricted to a certain number per month so you don't have endless options to contact people. Sales Navigator and Business Plus, currently give you 15 InMails per month.

The license fee for LinkedIn might be hefty, but it could get you a great return if you closed a few deals using this platform. Over time I'd assume that more features of LinkedIn's free version will be locked down to force professional users to switch over to the paid version.

LinkedIn Search

LinkedIn isn't just a business network, it's also a business-network search engine. Hence, similar rules apply to LinkedIn as they would to your search on e.g. Google Search. If you wanted to search for an exact phrase, put the search term in quotation marks, for example:
"Product Manager Mobile"

If you wanted to include another term in your search, use the word AND (must be written in capital letters). For example:
"Product Manager Mobile" AND Ecommerce
(Note that Ecommerce doesn't have to be in quotation marks).

If you want to combine two search phrases, you can use OR (must be in capital letters). For example:
Microsoft OR Google

Finally, by using a bracket you can make combinations:
"Product Manager" AND (Mobile OR Ecommerce)

These options can be very helpful when you want to narrow down your search results.

Sending invitations

In the spirit of being relevant and contextual as a sales professional, I find it annoying when I get a standard LinkedIn invitation from people who I have never heard of (e.g. *Hi, I'd like to connect with you on LinkedIn*). It takes 20 seconds to write a more personal message and it goes a long way to show the recipient some respect and courtesy.

Groups

LinkedIn has many special interest groups, some of which have hundreds of thousands of members. Even if you have no specific interest in groups, you should consider joining a few.

First of all, some groups actually have interesting and relevant content. Admittedly others have many members and a message board exploited by people who just want to sell their products. More importantly however, all members of the group will also appear in your search results, so you're widening the net in your searches. Additionally, you can send group members direct messages. Go to the group, click on the 'Members' link (which is on the top-right hand corner of the main group page), go to the contact you want to write to (alternatively you can also use the search bar) and look for the link 'Send message' next to the member's photo. The maximum number of groups you can join is limited to 50.

Privacy Settings

Connecting with others is great as you're building your network. The connections of your connections will also appear in your search results. Put differently, by connecting with someone, you're also getting (search) access to their connections. You can see all of their 1st degree connections.

The reverse is true too. Your connections can see all of your connections. If you're paranoid that your competitors might exploit that — provided you are connected with some of them — go to *Privacy & Settings*, then *'Select who can see your connections'* and change it to *'Only you'*. In this case, you've locked down access to your contacts.

Taking LinkedIn lead generation to the next level

LinkedIn is a business network and so there's a lot of sharing and updating going on. It's also an advertising platform, where you can put your product or company directly in front of users.

You can obviously participate on LinkedIn in different ways. Posting updates, writing blogs, commenting on other's updates or blogs and so on. You may even want to start your own group. Josh

Turner has written a book about this topic (*Connect: The Secret LinkedIn Playbook To Generate Leads, Build Relationships, And Dramatically Increase Your Sales*, Lioncrest Publishing, 2015) where he explains in some detail how you can turn special interest groups into lead generating tools. The key to all of this is to be helpful to others. Bluntly promoting your own product isn't going to work. If you can produce meaningful and interesting content, great. More about content strategy later in this chapter.

LinkedIn has so many aspects that this section is just scratching the surface. There's no doubt that using LinkedIn has become second nature to most sales professionals and knowing how to use LinkedIn as a sales tool is definitely important.

Industry websites/blogs

Techcrunch.com, for example, releases numerous articles about technology companies small and large. Filter your way through the articles to find relevant targets. Every industry has a 'TechCrunch'; in other words, a special interest website or a popular blog which can be used for lead generation.

Trade journals

Similar to websites/blogs, every industry has its own subject matter magazine where you may find additional leads and contacts (e.g. people quoted or named in interviews).

Trade shows

You could visit a trade show and collect business cards, but you may also want to look at the show's website. Sometimes they provide a full list of exhibitors and occasionally even visitors. In some instances, this can be your ready-made list for the taking. The same principle also applies to *conferences and meet-ups*.

Trade associations

Trade associations normally have a members' list or other contact lists you can use for lead generation.

Yellow Pages

Yellow Pages is particularly useful for finding smaller businesses (e.g. 'plumbers') in regional areas.

Events and trigger situations [outbound]

There is always something happening somewhere in your industry, so keep your eyes and ears open. Sales professionals are opportunity finders and the best see opportunities where others don't. Following the trade press, networking and staying tuned in with your connections is a precondition for identifying opportunities. Most sales professionals will do this automatically, although I'm not so sure that they always do it with a mindset of looking for new opportunities.

Referrals [in- and outbound]

Referrals can be a great source of new business and some experts suggest that the best sales professionals build their success at least in part on referrals. That said, anecdotal evidence suggests that not many salespeople actually engage in this strategy. Undoubtedly, finding prospects is one of the hardest activities in sales, so there's no rationale in missing out on comparatively low-hanging leads. Here are a few things to consider:

- **Just ask**
  Make asking for referrals a habit. Instead of waiting for the client to think about potential referrals, you could suggest companies or people to *them*. For example: 'I was wondering if you had any contacts at company ABC you

could introduce me to? We believe we'd have an interesting solution for them.' After which you could add: 'Or is there anybody else in your network you think might be interested in our product?' Ideally, you would like an introduction, but just receiving a referral contact is better than nothing and you can still use this to your advantage when you approach the referred contact. For example: 'Simon from XYZ is one of our clients and he recommended that I get in touch with you.'

- **Timing**
  In general, people are happy to give you a referral if they feel that you are credible and genuine. In other words, if they're satisfied with the work you delivered, they're normally comfortable helping you out. Your client's biggest risk is that you might jeopardise their relationship with their contact. Getting the timing right is crucial. If you ask too early you might give the impression that you've already moved on to the next deal before finishing the work for them. But if the deal falls through or you're in a fast-paced, transactional deal environment you might miss the window of opportunity when they would have the time and inclination to give you a referral.

- **Form your own lead army**
  Referrals can come from colleagues, friends and family, but in most cases it's not enough to sit and wait, you need to be proactive and tell your network what you are looking for and directly ask for their help. Usually, they are happy to oblige.

Partners [inbound]

Many companies generate substantial business from working with partners. For example, logistic companies which use each other's network to ship goods to places they are unable to reach with their own fleet. Another example is software agencies which work with software publishers to help them install and sell their software. There's a fine line between a partner and a supplier relationship. If you don't get access to the actual customer, you're a supplier rather than a partner. If you manage the referred customer relationship independently, then it's a partner-generated deal.

I can't think of many organisations where there isn't an opportunity to partner with other companies. All it takes to get the ball rolling is to open a conversation.

Online lead generation [inbound]

Your website is your online business card, but more importantly it's also an inbound lead generator. The more relevant and the more engaging you are, the greater the chances that somebody will submit an enquiry to you.

Basics

Make it easy for your customer to browse your website. Make sure you don't have a cluttered website that's difficult to navigate. User testing and a web analytics tool can give you some insights on what works and what doesn't. If you need some inspiration, go to high-traffic B2B websites and analyse how they manage their online portals. Don't forget to check out your competitors' websites, too.

Functional

The product you're selling needs to stand out and the description should be clear and simple. Working with professional visuals improves the appeal of the website. Put yourself into your customer's shoes and then let content and design follow.

Engaging

The content, which is basically your online pitch to your customer, should be interesting and entertaining to read. Just like when you're dealing with a customer directly, refrain from sounding too 'salesy' on your website — customers want meaningful and relevant information, not buzzwords. Writing good copy is not easy, so you may need help from a professional.

Accessible

Make it very easy for the prospect to contact you. Online forms are better than email links. Provide alternative contact options for convenience (phone, chat, physical business address).

Performance control

If you use a web analytics tool (e.g. Google Analytics), check the performance of your website on a regular basis, i.e. page views, unique visitors, conversion rates (if applicable) and any other data you're generating such as sign-ups. Test customer journeys to make sure everything works and is designed as it should be. Ideally your website is connected with your CRM tool so that you have all your leads, including the inbound leads, in one place.

Most companies link their systems so that an enquiry on the website creates an inbound lead in the CRM database. That's fairly easy to do and saves duplicate work like copy-pasting information. More advanced strategies link behavioural data with CRM accounts. For example, a prospect sends an enquiry through to a business which a) creates an account in the CRM system and b) 'cookies' the prospect's browser allowing them to identify the prospect on any return visit to the website. If the prospect comes back a day later to download a white paper and returns again the following day to have a look at the pricing table, the business would collect this information and send contextual information depending on where in the buying journey the prospect is. This marketing automation has gained significant traction in recent years. It allows the business to be more relevant in its messaging to the prospect and, as a result, close more deals.

Content strategy [inbound]

Content strategy overlaps in many ways with online lead generation, but it's more subtle in nature as there won't always be a direct link between input and output. Content could be a video blog discussing latest trends in your industry, created by you and your colleague. The video might feature a link to your website, but if the prospect is still in exploration mode, viewers might watch the video and then move on. Some weeks later, the same prospect comes through to your website and leaves an enquiry. They potentially clicked on one of your paid search ads on a search engine. Perceived success for your search engine campaign; failure for your video blog. Advanced tracking can help to mitigate this, but content might never be as direct-response as other inbound activities.

The idea of a content strategy is to increase awareness of your product by publishing engaging topics for your target audience. Anecdotal evidence suggests that small companies often start working on content, but don't have the required resources to keep it going and eventually end up abandoning it altogether. Hence, before you go down this path, reflect on whether you do have the time and resources to work on content.

If you can do it, do it. It can be hugely successful, particularly for small businesses. I know of one company which has been releasing weekly podcasts for many years discussing trends and news from their industry and it's become one of their most successful lead generating activities. It started very small, but they have grown it to the extent that there is now an audience of tens of thousands of listeners each week, however this did not happen overnight. It took many years to reach an audience of this size. Persistence and quality is key.

The most obvious places for content activities are blogs, video blogs (vlogs), podcasts, Twitter, Tumblr, Facebook and LinkedIn to name a few.

There are many different ways to generate leads, inbound as well as outbound. I've found that small companies often have a flagship lead-activity that works exceptionally well for them. I've already mentioned one small company that uses podcasts. I know of another that drives business by using Facebook in a witty and innovative way. In both cases, there's a personal affinity to the channel; the former just loves broadcasting while the latter loves the social nature of Facebook. They have each found and generated an audience and made it work for them. Their examples serve as a blueprint for smaller companies. With limited time and resources available, choices have to be made about where to engage, particularly when it comes to driving inbound leads. Personal affinity plays a role too, because if you feel uncomfortable with the nature of a channel, chances are you're not good at it and you're tempted to give up too easily.

The content you're producing doesn't have to be novel. I'd argue that most information is already out there. So, instead of trying to be very innovative, you can use what's out there and repackage it for your target audience. Content curation instead of content creation. If you're targeting construction companies in the south of England, could you repackage some of the news that's already out there? Could you use the main topics of a popular construction blog or website and adapt them for the local region? Curation is a much quicker process than investigating a topic from scratch.

Leads are like the seeds of the sales process. It's a small first step and it's still unclear whether anything will grow out of it. You can't rely on a single seed so you have to sow many seeds trusting that some will grow into opportunities and deals. The next step is to ensure that you cultivate only those leads that show promising qualities and separate them from the rest.

Qualifying leads

Qualifying leads means matching a lead against criteria to assess their relevance for your business. The BANT (Budget, Authority, Need and Time) concept introduced earlier is the most popular framework for this purpose. What does BANT mean in practice?

- **Budget**
  Your contact has the budget to buy from you

- **Authority**
  Your contact has the authority to make a buying decision

- **Need**
  Your contact has a need for your product

- **Time**
  Your contact has enough time/resources to conduct and complete the purchase

BANT is quite self-explanatory, but it's even more powerful when you reverse it. If the prospect has *no* budget, *no* authority (to sign the deal), *no* need and *no* time, the lead is worthless.

One or even multiple BANT issues won't kill a lead, but you've got work to do if you want to move it into your pipeline. For example, if the prospect customer doesn't have the budget to buy your product you need to find out if this is a permanent or a temporary situation. Institutional buyers often work against strictly defined annual budgets and need time to get investments approved. In this case, you might have to wait until the next budget year before you can close the deal.

Most sales professionals and sales teams don't use BANT as a hard and fast rule for qualifying leads. In most instances, it's largely down to the sales professional to qualify a lead or otherwise. For outbound leads, the bar is often as low as a prospect engaging in a conversation. Once the conversation is established, they drill deeper to get an understanding of the prospect's circumstances which loosely covers the BANT criteria. I can however say with some confidence that many sales professionals don't cover BANT criteria until very late in the sales process. One recent example I heard was a sales professional who worked with a junior contact at a large enterprise for months, believing (or rather hoping) that this person would be in a position to sign the deal. He had a rude awakening when it turned out not to be the case and it required a lot of intervention from senior management to rescue the deal.

Lead qualification is about understanding if there's a fit between your product and the company to whom you're selling. The 'Need' in BANT describes this, but it doesn't cover it in its entirety.

There will be situations where you realise that your product is the wrong fit for your prospect's requirements.

It's quite likely that you recognise this *before* your prospect does; firstly, because you normally know more about your product and your industry than your contact does, and secondly, because it's likely that you've been in similar situations before and therefore you can see it coming.

It's particularly challenging when the customer gets ever more excited about working with you because they believe your product is the solution to one of their business problems. You can decide to turn a blind eye and hope that it will work itself out, but I recommend being open and honest and discussing the issue with your prospect. To cling on to a bad deal means wasting time you could better spend elsewhere.

Some companies put a lead qualification scoring system in place. The scoring system could be as simple as having a scale of 1–5 for each BANT criteria where 5 is fully qualified and 1 is unqualified. When the entire sales process from end to end is done by the same person, scoring leads might seem like a waste of time, but you can use the scoring to retrospectively analyse your leads. It's quite likely that the lost deals performed poorly in the lead qualification scoring. Hence a little extra effort evaluating potential winners versus losers might go a long way towards improving your overall sales performance.

Lead-definition, lead-generation and lead-qualification are crucial in the sales process. Much of the remaining sales process depends on the quality of your leads which is why you need to avoid getting caught in the 'rubbish in (leads), rubbish out (lost opportunities)' trap.

The following case study demonstrates what happens if you ignore lead qualification.

....

Case Study: Never Fail To Qualify

A couple of years ago, Wendy took over as a managing director for a small software agency with four developers. The agency works with small to medium sized businesses to integrate licensed software from large publishers such as Microsoft. Like so many agencies in that field, the company's revenues came from a small number of high-value customers acquired over the years, mostly from referrals and a few from inbound enquiries.

After Wendy had settled into the job, she felt it was time to do more outbound sales work. She mainly approached companies which were in regional proximity to her office. She chose those where she thought she could get a friendly conversation going as she wanted to avoid spending time on cold-calls. Wendy didn't define leads as such, neither did she have a list of leads, instead she just went after businesses which she felt were a natural fit for her agency.

Once she had a meeting arranged she was eager to impress the prospect by showcasing the quality of her company's work. She also thought about areas where her company could help the prospect further. For example, when a prospect had a sales team she would demonstrate a CRM integration completed for another client as a real-life example, but first and foremost, Wendy was happy to get in front of potential customers. Wendy refrained from mentioning associated costs or asking for the prospects budget. She believed that investing in the relationship would eventually lead to winning new business.

Then one day she had a rude awakening. A prospect told her that whilst they loved all her suggestions, they had no budget, in fact they were in the process of cutting costs as their business went through a tough period. Alerted by this experience, she started to go through her pipeline one by one and started to qualify each opportunity in earnest. It turned out that with almost all of them there was either no budget or the prospect's price expectations were nowhere near Wendy's prices. In one embarrassing occasion, the prospect had thought the solution would be ten times cheaper than what Wendy needed to charge. Over the following weeks, her pipeline crashed like a house of cards.

Customers saying they have no budget for a new project isn't a surprise. When you do outbound work, your prospect hasn't set a bucket of money aside waiting to be spent on your product. Part of the job of a sales professional is to create demand, to demonstrate the value of the solution and to help the prospect find ways to finance it. One method to unlock funds is by showing how the solution improves the profitability (return on investment). Another tactic is to be mindful about thresholds. Many companies, particularly larger ones, have tight procedures in place for approving expenditure e.g. for purchases over £20,000. This means that sums below this line can be approved more easily, which might not always be practical, but sometimes you can use this to your tactical advantage.

For example, when you charge for your service in smaller instalments instead of one big lump sum.

Wendy's fundamental error, however, was that she failed to put a qualifying process in place. Process might even be too grand a word, for what is effectively just trying to understand if the prospect is in any position to buy from you or not. It has cost Wendy time, effort and lost deals which could have been used more productively.

....

Outbound

Outbound sales is synonymous with activity: contacting leads, selling, qualifying, asking for referrals, etc. The notion that sales is a numbers game is probably most apparent in doing outbound work. It is — to an extent — a mathematical exercise: you put five leads in and you get one deal out (if your 'conversion' rate happens to be 20 percent).

Numbers don't lie, but are numbers all there is to sales? There are a few trends that are changing the face of sales significantly.

Firstly, more and more sales jobs take on a consultative nature, meaning deals are less transactional and, consequently, the customer expects more of a relationship with the sales professional than someone who just facilitates the technicalities of a deal. This is amplified by changes in the market like monthly subscription fees (technology) instead of a one-off license fee; leasing machinery instead of high-value purchases; and freelancing instead of permanent employment. Closing the deal is, therefore, only the start of a business relationship and not the end of a transactional deal. The customer's business needs to be 'earned' on a continuous basis.

Secondly, technology changes the way we communicate. LinkedIn allows you to build an online network that would have been hard to manage previously. Your smartphone is your computer in your pocket. Sharing information has never been easier because everybody can tweet, blog and broadcast about their field of expertise. *Connecting* has never been more important for sales professionals.

Finally, consultative sales cycles tend to be longer and prospect discussions are generally more thorough. Even if you're not closing a deal, in consultative sales situations you're positioning yourself as an expert and, if you've left an impression with your contact, they'll remember you when the time is right.

In the light of these trends there's more to sales than just hitting the phone. It requires you to engage in the wider context of problem solving (consultative sales), technology, social networks as well as long-term relationship building. Ultimately it requires you to be flexible in your sales approach: understanding the importance of numbers (leads) as well as the dynamics of your sales environment.

Cold Calling

For most people the thought of making cold calls sends a shiver down their spine. 'Put me in a room with a potential customer and I'm at my best, but don't make me cold call.' You've probably heard salespeople say this or something very similar. There's widespread fear about making cold calls and it can be a daunting experience if you haven't had any training or practice.

With skill, preparation and attitude, cold-calling can become an extremely successful endeavour.

But let's first explore why so many people find it so difficult.

Low success rates

In the first instance just getting hold of someone is hard enough. Depending on the quality of the leads list and the contact details on record, the success rate for reaching anyone relevant on your first attempt can be very low. It can be frustrating to dial one number after the other only to get stuck in voicemail or hear that the person you'd like to speak to is in a meeting or simply doesn't want to take your call. Trying to get in touch with useful contacts is a bit like turning rocks, hoping to find gems underneath. Often you'll have to try and try before you get to the gem.

Dealing with rejection

Sometimes you'll be turned down flat. You might get a rude response or the phone will be hung up. Unless you have some experience in cold calling, you'll find it quite hard to handle this kind of rejection.

Dull task

Making good cold calls requires a wide range of skills, but getting into a rut of dialling number after number and logging calls into your CRM system can get draining.

So why do we bother making cold calls at all? Calling does have a few major benefits over other methods: Firstly, it's cheap: you can make a call from pretty much *anywhere* and you can make *many calls* in a day. Secondly, it's a two-way conversation so you can ask questions or react immediately to a prospect's objections. Thirdly, it's a good way to build rapport. Only a personal meeting will give you a better platform for establishing a relationship, but they are also much more expensive.

Here's a little personal experience of mine. Back in high school I wanted to get a summer job in Vienna, Austria, but it was already May and most of the jobs were gone. What's worse, my girlfriend had found a job so I was faced with the prospect of spending the summer far away at my parent's home in the countryside. I went to the local post office (this was before mobiles became ubiquitous), got into a phone booth, armed myself with the yellow pages and started dialling numbers, selling myself to employers. I called around 300 numbers over the course of a few hours. Most of the calls turned into rejections of course, but a few people were interested. One job was immediately open and I was offered an interview. I ended up working at the reception of a small B&B in central Vienna and I loved it. I don't think I could have achieved that in any other way than by calling them. At the time, I had no idea that this was 'cold calling', but with hindsight it was my first proper sales experience. Being under pressure helped too.

Here's another, very recent example from a friend of mine, Peter, who tried to reach a senior marketing contact at one of the big telecoms companies in the UK. Peter isn't trained in cold-calling and he's relatively inexperienced, but he gave it a go.

First attempt calling the switchboard:

'Can I speak to somebody in marketing please?'
'I'm sorry we can't put you through unless we have a name. Do you know who you want to speak to?'
'Erm...sorry, I'd just like to offer a promotion to the marketing team.'
'I'm afraid I can't put you through.'
'Thanks.'

Peter goes on LinkedIn, finds the name of an executive at the company and calls back:

'Can you put me through to John Smith please?'
'Thank you.' (Puts him through)
'John Smith.'
'Hi John, Peter here, I'm calling from XYZ, we're the market leader in hampers and gift sets in the UK. We know your customers love our products from our market research and we'd like to offer you a promotion.'

'Erm...Ok, that wouldn't be me handling this. Send me an email and I'll forward it to my colleague.'

Peter sent an email to John detailing the offer with low expectation of getting anywhere. Two weeks later he was contacted by the responsible marketing manager, Tina. Four weeks later the promotion went ahead. What's to be learned from this experience? The cold call wasn't perfect, but it was genuine and honest. The way the offer was presented wasn't ideal. He gave up a little early in trying to find out who would be in charge. The key message though is that action pays off. If you never try, you'll never know.

How many cold calls do you need to make? It depends amongst other things on your deal target and your cold-calling success rate.

Say you have a target of 60 deals for a nine-month period and you forecast that you can close 30 deals from inbound leads. So the other half, the other 30 deals, have to come from outbound activities. Let's assume that outbound means exclusively cold calling. If your conversion rate from lead to deal is 20 percent you need to work through at least 150 leads (30 deals divided by a 20 percent conversion rate results in 150 leads).

Obviously, you also need to be mindful of the average time it takes for a deal to close. If it takes on average 90 days from the first contact to the actual signing of a deal, you need to have finished all cold calling by the end of the sixth month to have 90 days left to hit your deal target by the end of the ninth month.

Where do you get your conversion rate from? Once you've worked through a good number of leads over a certain period you can divide your number of deals closed through the total number of leads and the result will be your conversion rate.

If you find cold-calling daunting, here are a few things to make it easier for yourself:

Relevance

Before you make a cold call, remind yourself of all of the reasons why your product is useful for your prospect. In what way can it help the prospect be more successful? It sounds obvious, but it might not be top of your mind when you're desperately chasing the next deal and you're under pressure to hit your deal target. Have a good reason to call and your confidence will rise and so will your success rate.

Abundance

Abundance means that in most markets there are almost infinite sales opportunities. If this doesn't convince you, look at it from another angle: What would happen if everyone in your target market were to place an order with you today? You'd probably struggle to fulfil even a fraction of them. In the context of cold-calling this means that if your next call isn't successful, there are plenty of other leads remaining who will want to do business with you.

Persist

It's easy to find excuses why today isn't a good day for cold calling, but new leads are fundamental for a healthy sales pipeline so persist and make those calls regardless of how many excuses you might find.

Habitual

Set aside time for cold-calling and set yourself an outbound target per week, month, and quarter. You can certainly retain some flexibility and shift some activity from one week to another, but one of the biggest threats to a healthy, continuous revenue stream is the lack of continuous prospecting to refill the sales pipeline.

Script

If you cold-call regularly, you won't necessarily need a script, but otherwise it's really helpful to have a written structure before you get on the call. It certainly doesn't mean you should read the script

Driving Sales Results

line by line, which would sound odd and artificial, but having a tried and tested approach for your calls makes for a better flow.

Develop a list of questions that you want to have answered by the end of a cold-call — circumstances permitting. Scripts should also cover objection handling. There's normally a short list of frequent objections and having a solid response to those is going to help tremendously during the call. If you think scripting sounds a bit odd, keep in mind that even experienced stand-up comedians script their shows in minute detail only to make you believe it is all improvised when they perform.

Planning is important, but in reality calls can take many unforeseen turns. Good communications skills help as well as simply giving your undivided focus to the call. One key rule: refrain from using your computer while speaking on the phone. Concentrate on listening, asking the right questions, and taking notes.

Icebreaker

Cold calls are easier if you have an icebreaker. For example, I have a German accent so whenever I make a cold call in English I apologise for my accent and explain that I'm an Austrian who ended up in London. It removes any preconceived ideas my prospects might have (e.g. 'Where's this guy calling from?') and normally triggers a friendly conversation. I've found this to be a good icebreaker for me.

My preferred route for an icebreaker is to find similarities with the prospect, like mutual acquaintances, similar career background, or the same university — anything that's relevant and credible. The go-to places for finding such hints are obviously your social networks like LinkedIn. Doing a quick online check takes only a few minutes, but it can make a call so much smoother and it's a proven fact that people prefer to do business with people with whom they share similarities.

Below are a few more thoughts on cold-calling and on prospecting in general.

- **Aim high**
  Try to get in touch with people on the C-level (decision makers and key budget holders). They may not be the people who personally negotiate the deal, but they're the ones who have the authority to sign off a deal. If those decision makers refer you down to a more junior manager, that's fine. It's often perceived as a recommendation by their seniors to give your offering serious consideration. Conversely, if you start too low in the hierarchy, you may end up with someone who was never entitled to make a decision on your product in the first place. It's then much harder to work your way up to the decision maker.

- **Understand roles**
  The VP of Sales will be interested in increasing revenues. The CFO will be interested in managing costs. So your pitch needs to be tailored to the function of the executive you're calling.

- **Know the facts**
  'About Us' on company websites will normally give you an overview of the company's activities. Other news can either be found on search engines or on the corporate section of the website. It's nice to have a contextual element in your call along the lines of 'I read in your last statement that you're planning to upgrade your IT,' or small talk: 'I heard you're moving offices.' It shows that you're knowledgeable and that you care.

- **Document what's working and what doesn't**
  Either by iterating your sales script or by keeping a cold-calling journal.
  Analyse, iterate and test.

Cold emailing

Emails (including messages on social networks like LinkedIn) are an alternative for getting in touch with your prospects. (Cold-emailing as discussed here is sending *individual* emails from your email account and not mass-emailing). Email is often the only option when you fail to contact someone over the phone. Anecdotal evidence suggests that the bigger the company, the harder it is to reach your target by phone. It tends to be easier to reach the owner of a small company than the marketing director of a blue-chip company. You can also use a combination of emailing and calling by initially sending a brief introduction via email and then following up with a phone call.

Here are a few best practice tips for cold emailing:

- **Subject line**
  The sole purpose of the subject line is to encourage your prospect to open the email. You need to produce something interesting and relevant whilst staying within the limits of professionalism. You can test for yourself what subject lines get you a reaction by enabling read-receipts on your email — or CRM — program. The challenge is to find a short subject line that captures the imagination of your prospect. In general, the more personal and the more contextual, the higher the chance that the email will actually be opened.

- **Trust**
  The email address has to be sent from a trusted source and mustn't have any spelling errors. In the body of the email address you have to provide your full contact details, including a social network link like LinkedIn.

- **Keep it short**
  Put yourself into your prospect's shoes: What kind of email would you open, read and respond to? Cold emails should

only contain a few lines in the main text to get the key message across:

- ◦ Introduce yourself (1 sentence)
- ◦ Introduce the company (1 sentence)
- ◦ Describe the proposal and the value for the prospect (1-2 sentences)

If this feels too brief for you, test long versus short emails and see if you can detect a difference in response rates. If in doubt, always use your prospect as the reference point and write in a style you think they'd find interesting and engaging. In my own experience, long-winded, salesy emails are near useless, whilst short ones generate a response.

- • **Personal**
The more generic your email, the lower the chances of it being successful. Show the reader that you care about their business. This can be something bespoke like: 'We have analysed your marketing strategy and found five ways to improve your performance. Can we share our findings with you?' Anything that makes your email more personal is going to help you.

Inbound

Inbound leads are heavenly! Somebody contacts you and all that needs to be done is to send the order form through. Well, if only it was that straightforward (sometimes it is). Unfortunately, not every inbound enquiry is a quality lead, so the first task is to separate the good from the bad.

Spam

Spam reaches you in all forms, some of it will be filtered by your Internet Service Provider and your own systems, but in most cases some manual intervention will still be needed to clean your inbound leads.

General enquiries

General enquiries are not sales leads. If you get many of them through your sales links, you may want to revisit your inbound contact form to make sure they are being pointed in the right direction. For general enquiries, there should be a separate contact form on your website.

Sales leads

There are few things more enjoyable in a sales professional's job than getting great inbound leads.

Maintaining a steady stream of inbound leads is by no means a free lunch. It requires significant marketing efforts as described in this chapter under *Generating leads*, but once the inbound operation is set in place, there's no active role for sales to play until the lead comes through your systems. Sit back, relax and enjoy.

Sorting

Sorting means deciding what to do next with your leads. Some leads might go straight into the pipeline; others will require more work and some might be unqualified or closed. Figure 5 describes this process and whilst at first glance the chart looks a bit complicated, it's actually quite straightforward.

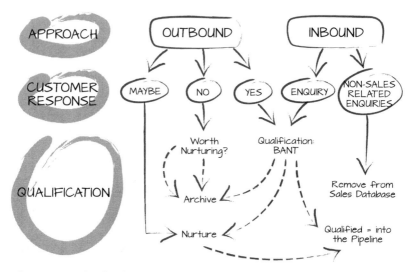

Figure 5: Sorting leads

Fully qualified leads are converted into opportunities and moved into the sales pipeline. For the rest, there are a few options:

Delete

Delete leads that are obviously not worthy to be worked on *now* or in the *future*, such as customer service enquiries, charity requests, sales emails (oh the irony!) and spam. If they're genuine, respond to the enquirer, but eventually *all* of these unrelated contacts need to be *deleted* from your sales database. They aren't relevant now and never will be. If you keep them on record in your CRM system it will mess up your database and make your contact list that much harder to use when you decide to revisit archived contacts in the future.

Driving Sales Results

Outbound leads are normally less likely to produce duds, provided the lead generation process has been handled diligently.

Archive

Archive or 'park' any other lead when it's a genuine sales lead, but doesn't meet your qualification criteria. Examples are enquiries from countries you don't ship to or enquiries for product ranges you don't stock. These leads have an industry context and some of them might turn into business, but not in the foreseeable future.

Nurture

Nurture leads when they haven't passed your BANT qualification, but might still turn into a deal at some point. Instead of completely dropping the contact keep them on your nurturing list. Below are a few examples why you'd keep leads in the nurturing bucket (mostly they're related to the BANT qualification criteria).

Budget

The hotel likes your product, but doesn't have the budget to buy from you (now).

Authority

The retailer is a great fit for your product, but you don't have any senior stakeholder buy-in and you can't progress with your junior contacts.

Need

The large telecoms company is tied up in a contract with one of your competitors for another two years.

Time

The printing company is interested in your new technology, but isn't taking on any new projects until they've completed a factory move and launched a new market.

The lead issues described above might go away in the future so instead of just archiving them, you can nurture these contacts until they're ready to buy. Of course, that might never happen so put a milestone into your calendar such as: 'if the budget for our product has not been allocated by January of next year, disqualify the lead'. There's always a risk that nurturing a lead won't yield results, but considering how much effort it takes to find and engage with leads in the first place, it's worth putting some low-touch effort into nurturing with a view to eventually closing a deal.

Nurturing is just another way of saying that you will stay in touch in a meaningful way. To this end, make sure that your approach is interesting and relevant. Large companies often have a dedicated nurturing programme and if you haven't come across one, sign up to a B2B leader in your industry and wait for the communication to come through. Usually it's email. Nurturing isn't just for big companies. Small companies are also perfectly capable of quality nurturing and will potentially do an even better job because they tend to have a more personal relationship with their contacts.

There's also a potential overlap between nurturing and generating inbound leads (see *Generating leads* in Chapter 3). If you're producing and publishing content with the aim of getting leads (e.g. blogs, newsletters, websites, tweets and LinkedIn updates) you may also use this content for nurturing purposes. Whilst nurturing is important, you cannot devote the same amount of time and attention to nurturing as you would to selling, simply because you have a much higher chance of closing *qualified* leads. That's why they need to be given priority in your sales process.

Here are a few nurturing ideas:

- **Newsletters**
  Keep your contacts updated on product, industry, market and company news. This doesn't have to be a shiny, elab-

Driving Sales Results

orately-designed newsletter. It can be a text-based email. The important thing is that it contains information your contacts will find interesting.

- **Phone**

  For strategic contacts (e.g. the biggest prospects in your market) you should check in by phone every few months. The advantage of calling is that you can retain a two-way conversation. Besides general updates, the conversation can be more informal — even a little industry gossip when appropriate. This type of nurturing can also be likened to networking because strategic contacts are likely to be well connected in your industry.

- **Other ideas**
  - Meet-ups, presentations, conferences, trade shows and industry events normally attract a lot of industry contacts, so it's an efficient way to get through your nurturing list.

  - Direct mailing
    Direct mailing can be relatively expensive in comparison to email. The most personal (and potentially effective) direct mailing though is a Christmas card with a few lines.

  - Blogs
    Good blogs generate subscribers and unlike emails might actually spread and reach beyond the contacts you have on your list.

  - Updates on Twitter, LinkedIn, Facebook, etc.

Even if you work in a small organisation, don't discard the idea of nurturing just because it sounds complicated and time consuming. You can apply a pragmatic approach and pick a few tactics mentioned above (or create new ones) and give your nurturing contacts an update every couple of months.

Create an opportunity

Hallelujah! If you've turned a lead into an opportunity, pat yourself on the shoulder. It's not a deal (yet), but an achievement in itself as every opportunity is a potential deal contender. I use the term *opportunity* here for any record that sits in the pipeline.

Review

So, let's review what we've discovered. Basically, every business needs leads; every company needs prospects to turn into deals which means revenue for the company, and hopefully profitability so the business thrives.

We've explored defining the different kinds of leads: for instance warm/cold; inbound/outbound. We've worked on ways of generating leads (included the dreaded cold-calling). And we've analysed how to qualify and nurture those leads.

The next step, which I cover in the next chapter, is understanding, analysing and managing the potential business that's in your pipeline.

CHAPTER 4

The pipeline

Sales is a bit like gambling. Instead of placing a wager on a sports game, you bet that an opportunity turns into a winning deal. Your pipeline represents the total of all of your sales bets. Some of them will pay off, some of them won't. Placing a bet in the real world means parting with money; for sales, it means parting with your valuable time — time that you could have invested elsewhere. So, you have to be aware that with every account in your pipeline there's an opportunity cost as you could be working on something else instead.

Now, there's a significant difference between gambling and selling. Gambling is down to probabilities, selling is down to the quality of the sales professional. You are, however, working with finite resources (time) and selling requires you to take a certain level of risk. You can't know in advance if an opportunity will close as a deal or not. Your pipeline will reflect all of your choices. The *chosen ones* are the opportunities you selected, because they look most promising. Managing your pipeline means reviewing each opportunity, evaluating the next step in the conversation with the buyer, but also looking at the bigger picture — the overall numbers and the aggregated view on your sales performance.

Creating opportunities

When new opportunities come into your pipeline you should record a few data points.

- **Expected close date**
  The expected close date might not be particularly accurate when you've only just begun your conversation with a new contact, but a rough date will suffice for a start.

- **Next task**
  It's a very powerful tactic to close every conversation with an agreement on what the next step will be and when it's due. Ideally, you should put a reminder into your diary and, if appropriate, send your prospect a calendar invitation.

- **Assign a value**
  Most sales professionals will assign a monetary value to their opportunities. Alternatively, you can also use other values like order size or service agreement. This will allow you to calculate and forecast the total value of your pipeline. It's up to you how many stages you want to use in your pipeline, but usually there are three main ones:

  - *Early Stage*
    Gathering all requirements and establishing a way of working with your contact.

  - *Advanced Stage* (Proposition)
    Making and refining the offer.

  - *Late Stage* (Negotiation)
    Closing and contract negotiation.

New opportunities usually come in at Early Stage, but that's not a hard and fast rule. Some opportunities will progress so quickly that you can immediately put them into Late Stage. That typically happens when a prospect needs your solution quickly and has already made up its mind before they even contacted you.

Eventually an opportunity exits the pipeline as a deal won or as an opportunity lost. The pipeline should not have any permanent residents and removing stalled opportunities is part of good pipeline housekeeping. Opportunities are lost at every stage, but the highest drop-out rate is normally within the early stages, simply because that's where the match-making happens. Most of the details of a potential deal emerge in the early stages and that's when seller and buyer identify potential blockers that might make a deal unviable.

When you lose an opportunity you don't have to abandon it for good. You may decide to put it back into your nurturing programme, similar to what we discussed earlier about leads. Just because somebody's not buying from you now doesn't mean they won't buy from you in the future.

Managing the process

Every sales professional works towards closing deals, but deals are only the result of the work put in beforehand. You can't control your results, but you can control your input. This input is best managed by a range of *lead* indicators that your pipeline produces. Those performance indicators give you an idea about your performance long before the actual results (deals) come through.

But before you can manage and analyse a pipeline you need to actually *have* one in the first place. In other words, you need a place where you document your sales activities. Without any records, there's no pipeline and without a pipeline there's no sales management. This is where a CRM system comes into place. If you're not familiar with CRM go online and do some basic research. This market is vast and fragmented and there are hundreds of solutions available. Sales CRM's are a bit like bookkeeping-software for sales professionals. You could use Microsoft Excel for bookkeeping and to record your sales activities, but chances are that it's not very convenient and ends up being messy. A CRM prompts you into following a process. Moving leads from one stage to the next (or sorting them out), helping you keep on top of your activities and tasks.

Using a good CRM system is a bit like driving a nice car: a nice car doesn't necessarily make you a better driver, but your journey is probably more enjoyable and safer. Using a CRM system doesn't improve your selling skills, but your sales work will be better structured and documented.

CRM systems come in all flavours and it's hard to compare them. I'm not aware of a comprehensive comparison that has been conducted and there are too many parameters to consider — your personal requirements and those of your company. I have personally used Salesforce for many years and found their reporting functionality exceptional. For small companies or individuals, the complexity of Salesforce can be a little challenging. There's also a few free solutions out there. Zoho and Hubspot are among them. I've recently used Hubspot's free CRM and whilst its dashboard is very simplistic, it's quick and easy to set up.

Here are a few criteria I have found to be important for your CRM:

- Create contacts and accounts. Accounts are usually companies or organisations. For example, John Smith [contact] of ABC Company [account].
- Log calls, emails, meetings and activities.
- Assign progress to the account/opportunity.
  For example: Early Stage/Advanced Stage/Late Stage (alternative stages are fine too as long as they reflect the timeline above).
- Reports
  Reports are *the most important reason* why you'd want to use a CRM tool in the first place. If the reporting functionality isn't rich, you'll limit your ability to manage the pipeline.

Driving Sales Results

- Extra functionality
  Import and export data. The export function is useful should you ever change CRM systems. The import function is needed to batch-import leads into your system. Even creating a small number of leads manually — let's say just 20 — is painful.

- Accessibility
  Your sales CRM should be accessible from mobile devices (smartphone, tablet) as well as on your desktop.

- Reference customers
  Don't be the guinea pig. Have a look at the provider's reference list and even speak with someone who's using it already.

- Usability
  Some CRM suppliers cater for the largest companies in the world and, as a result, their systems have become incredibly complex because they have to comply with the requirements of big bureaucracies. Whilst there's often a scaled-down version for smaller businesses, the complexity can still be daunting and you may also need some setup, maintenance and training assistance. Usability is important, but it can't be traded for functionality. Some solutions are nothing more than a glorified contact management system, with very limited sales specific functionality, which defeats the purpose of using a CRM system.

- Scalability
  Most cloud-based systems can be scaled quite easily, but you may want to understand the implications of adding more users to the system.

- Compatibility
  Adding plug-ins, for example with social networks such as LinkedIn, can make working with your CRM system more convenient and efficient. This is really one to watch out for as smaller CRM providers may lack compatibility.

Today, the tools for selling go above and beyond using a CRM solution. Some sales professionals talk about their 'sales stack', a jargon borrowed from the technology world, describing layers of components used to building a software solution. In a similar fashion, sales professionals use a range of tools to build their own sales solution. The ones I've used are Sidekick (free) for tracking purposes, LinkedIn for finding contacts, Salesloft for building leads lists, Salesforce and Hubspot for CRM. This space has become increasingly dynamic in recent years and I'm in no doubt that more is to come.

Understanding, analysing and managing your pipeline

Recording sales data and activities is important, but it's near worthless if you're not using the information you gather to improve your performance. If you're spending time logging your data you should also spend time analysing it.

One of the best nuggets a CRM system can produce are the aforementioned lead indicators. They're critical because there's obviously a time-lag between your sales-input and your deal-output. What exactly is a lead indicator? One example is your level of sales activity. Look at it this way, your CRM gives you the ability to track your activities, just like a fitness app does. If you know that your average activity per month is 100 customer calls, meetings, follow-ups, cold calls (bundled together) and you did 120 this month, there's a good chance you'll see a positive impact on your performance in future months. Activity doesn't equate to quality, of course, but in combination with other indicators it can give you a good benchmark on where you stand. Managing your pipeline means managing your lead indicators because your current deal performance is the result of your previous sales work.

In some industries, sales results might lag behind for as long as a year or more until the full impact becomes visible. The longer the time lag, the fewer options you'll have to fix your pipeline in the short term.

For this very reason, lead indicators are not the only truth, as no single indicator will give you the full picture of your pipeline.

The shape of your pipeline

What's the ideal shape of a pipeline? If we follow the sales funnel analogy with many opportunities at the top and fewer towards the bottom we'd expect to see this represented in our ideal pipeline. This shape is shown in Figure 6.

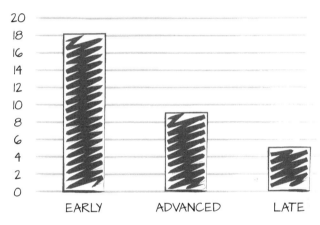

Figure 6: Perfectly shaped pipeline

Examples of problematic pipelines

Clearly, your sales activities can't always be linear so you'd expect different shapes at different times. In Figures 7 and 8 there are two pipelines which have slightly gone out of shape. In Figure 7 each stage has the same number of opportunities, which is worrying since you lose opportunities from stage to stage so you'd expect that once the current Early Stage opportunities move to the Late Stage, it'll be a fraction of the size of the current Late Stage. It's an even worse scenario in Figure 8 where the Late Stage has the most opportunities. If your pipeline has a short sales cycle, for example, four weeks, this issue can be fixed easily as you just need to focus on getting new opportunities into your pipeline. However, as mentioned before, with longer sales cycles there won't be a quick fix and your late stage opportunities can dry out very quickly once the current late-stagers have left the pipeline.

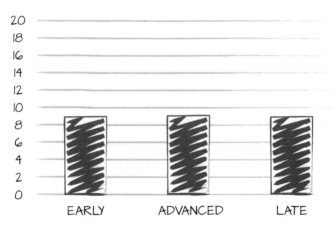

Figure 7: Missing the curve

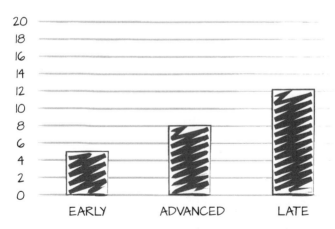

Figure 8: Wrong way round

Figure 9 and Figure 10 are different as there is only one stage of the three that is of concern. In Figure 9 there are too few Advanced Stage opportunities and in Figure 10 there are too few Late Stage opportunities. There can be different explanations, but, in principle, it'll either be the result of too little input (not enough leads qualified in that period) or higher than normal churn (maybe low quality opportunities that had to be cleaned out from the pipeline; this could also hint to a lead qualification issue or a batch of low quality leads).

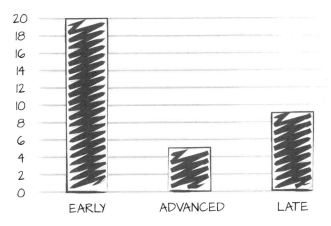

Figure 9: Not enough Advanced Stage Opportunities

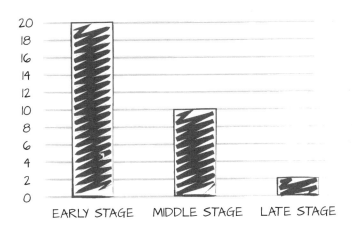

Figure 10: Not enough Late Stage Opportunities

Detailed pipelines

The pipeline shape will give you an instant health check, but in order to get more detail you can break down opportunities by territory and by product groups (provided, of course, that you have multiple territories and more than one product group).

Table 3 illustrates how the pipeline can be split into territories.

	Early	Advanced	Late	Total
North	3	3		6
West	15	4	2	21
East	2	2	1	5
Central	3	1		4
Export	4	3	1	8
Total	**27**	**13**	**4**	**44**

Table 3: Opportunities by territory

Conversion/Win rate

The conversion rate is the percentage of deals won divided by the number of opportunities in each stage as shown in table 4. The conversion rate is particularly useful in predicting the number of deals you're getting from your current pipeline.

All opportunities which reached	Opportunities created between 1 January and 31 June	Deals closed by 31 October	Conversion
Early Stage	165		20%
Advanced Stage	100	33	33%
Late Stage	55		60%

Table 4: Conversion rates of pipeline stages

How exactly do you calculate the conversion rate? You need to define a certain period (for example, six months as shown above) and then count all of the opportunities that have reached the respective stages. As for the deals, you may want to extend the period to allow for all or at least most of the deals from this period to come through. You should have a rough idea about the length of your sales cycle which should give you an idea. Please note that in the example above, the deal number (33) always remains the same.

Pipeline size

If you're wondering how many opportunities you should have in your pipeline, follow the calculation below. However, the actual pipeline size will always depend on the complexity of the product, how much support you're getting from other teams, and how much time you spend on selling as well as the current market conditions.

Example:

- Deal target: 36 deals for the upcoming current financial year
- Sales cycle: 100 days
- Conversion rate from opportunity creation to deals won is 20%
- 36 deals divided by the conversion rate (20%) gives you a target pipeline of 180 opportunities for the entire year

$$\frac{36 \ (\text{deal target})}{20\%} = 180$$

- If you divide 180 opportunities by 12 months you get 15, equal to the number of opportunities you need to add each month.
- In table 5, we move the opportunities through the three-month lifecycle, resulting in three deals each month.
  - 15 new opportunities are added in January
  - After one month (in February), six are lost hence you still have nine remaining
  - After another month (March), you successfully close three deals
- In this example, the pipeline size should be around 30 opportunities in any given month (29 to be precise).

The main message here isn't to scientifically calculate how your pipeline size will look like in December, but more importantly that your pipeline most certainly needs to be bigger than the monthly opportunity number would suggest. In other words, if you need to work through 180 opportunities in 12 months, your monthly target would be 15. However, with three-month sales cycles, your pipeline will have to contain around 30 opportunities at any one time, so twice as much as the monthly target would suggest.

	Jan	Feb	Mar	Apr	May	Jun	Jul	Aug	Sep	Oct	Nov	Dec	Pipeline size	Deals
Jan	15										5	9	29	3
Feb	9	15										5	29	3
Mar	5	9	15										29	3
Apr		5	9	15									29	3
May			5	9	15								29	3
Jun				5	9	15							29	3
July					5	9	15						29	3
Aug						5	9	15					29	3
Sep							5	9	15				29	3
Oct								5	9	15			29	3
Nov									5	9	15		29	3
Dec										5	9	15	29	3
													180	**36**

Table 5: Pipeline size

Activity rate

CRM systems like Salesforce allow you to track your sales activities such as customer meetings, calls, emails, events, etc. — basically any kind of customer contact.

Being active doesn't necessarily mean being effective, but combined with the right skillset, activity will generally lead to results. Low levels of customer activity may not mean 'laziness', but could be an indicator that you're not spending enough time selling. I'm an absolute fan of the activity report, illustrated in Figure 11, as it's one of the best lead indicators I know to evaluate my sales work.

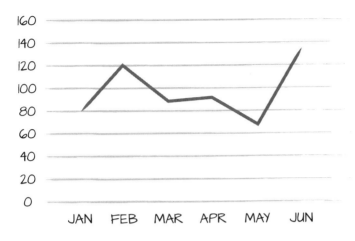

Figure 11: Pipeline activity levels

Fresh pipeline indicator

Imagine two pipelines looking identical (see table 6): The first one (A) contains 50 opportunities, of which 30 opportunities have been added over the last month, whilst the other one (B) also contains 50 opportunities of which only 5 have been added over the last month.

	A	B
Opportunities in the pipeline	**50**	**50**
Opportunities older than 3 months	20	45
Opportunities created this month	30	5
Opportunity turnover	**60%**	**10%**

Table 6: Pipeline turnover

In terms of the topline (50 opportunities) both look identical, but in their structure they are quite different. Whilst for A, the pipeline is relatively fresh with 30 new opportunities; for B, the pipeline consists of mainly old opportunities (45).

Driving Sales Results

Why would you end up with an old pipeline? For the same reason many people don't sell stocks after they've made a massive loss in the hope that the stock price might come back. Sometimes they do come back, but sometimes cutting your losses and investing elsewhere is more lucrative. The same applies to your pipeline when you're hanging on to lost opportunities.

Conclusions

There's no question that you need to record your sales data somewhere. You may as well do it with a decent CRM system which allows you to analyse your sales activities. It'll help you find more clarity on the status quo, so there are fewer surprises for you and the people with whom you're working. It's the basis for proper forecasting which is crucial for all companies, but most important for those companies where an order triggers a chain reaction across the organisation (e.g. manufacturing).

In this context, analysing the aggregate performance of the pipeline is like zooming out and looking at the bigger picture. Zooming in on the other hand is required to figure out the next step you need to take to close an individual deal. The following section is about zooming in and what methods you can apply to close deals quicker.

Closing deals

Closing deals somehow suggests that everything comes down to this pinnacle moment when you either win or lose the customer at the 11th hour. In reality, most deals develop over a period of time and then lean towards one or the other side before the final decision is made. The buyer will normally not just evaluate the product, but also you as a person to understand if they want to work with you or not. If you're representing an organisation, you'll be on the spot for the entire company. That's where great sales people make a difference, because they give the buyer a better experience and, more importantly, a taste of the work to be expected from you and your company.

Closing skills matter when it comes to handling buyer uncertainties and when trying to draw the sales process to an end. Handling objections requires the ability to read and understand a buyer. Make sure you fully grasp what the objection is. For tactical reasons the buyer will often be very selective with the information they give away and use all kinds of strategies to get the best deal possible. Understanding the real reason for objections is important because you can then distinguish whether or not there is a genuine deal breaker as opposed to the buyer testing your limits.

The most challenging objections are those which are important to the buyer and very hard, or even impossible, for you to accommodate. For instance, the customer might ask for a reduced purchasing price which, despite all best intentions, is unaffordable for your business. If lowering your price is not an option, could you add extra value to the deal instead? Maybe an additional feature which would normally come in at an extra cost? If you're selling a service, can you change the fee structure or grant a free trial period? Can the offer be altered (e.g. remove features) to change the price? Can the payments dates be changed to accommodate your customer? It's important to note that most buyers work within strict budget cycles and you may only secure a deal if you can help your prospect split the cost over two or more budget periods.

Whatever the solution, creativity in slicing and dicing the deal can eventually lead to a satisfying solution for both sides.

Alternatively, if it becomes clear that there is an insurmountable hurdle, it might be worth accepting defeat and moving on. If, for example, price remains the issue and all angles have been tried and tested, there comes a point where you may be better off cutting your losses. Take a step back and summarise the key benefits of your solution to the prospect one final time and if you can't reach agreement just let it go.

Closing a deal is all about timing and the experienced sales professional knows when to make a move. It's about asking the right questions and taking the initiative. Don't think of it as a clever technique that will make the buyer sign on the dotted line, but instead as a way to move the conversation to a successful conclusion. Unlike the rest of the sales process, at this stage it's not about asking open questions. What you really want is to trigger a decision by working with closing questions.

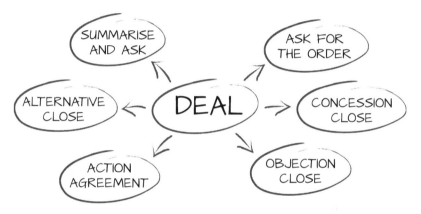

Figure 12: Closing techniques. Source: David Jobber and Geoff Lancaster (2009)

The closing questions shown in Figure 12 are explained in more detail below:

- **Ask for the business**
  'Can I send you the contract?'
  'When can we start delivering/implementing/working?'

- **Concession close**
  'If I gave you a discount for the first three months, can we shake hands on the deal?'

'If I rescheduled our engineers so that they could start working on your project next week, would you sign the contract today?'

- **Objection close**
  The objection close refers to a buyer objection that has been raised during the sales conversation:
  'If we provided you with evidence that our solution is cheaper to operate than your current solution, would you buy it?'
  'We could come on Monday and show you how we work. If you're happy with our service, would you hire us?'

- **Action agreement**
  Refers to a situation where the deal can only be closed when a task is completed.
  'We'll provide you with the technical specifications by Tuesday of next week. Can we send you the contract afterwards and aim to get it signed by Friday?'
  'I'll get back to you tomorrow on the open questions. Provided you're happy with the answers, can we start next Monday?'

- **Alternative close**
  Very similar to the Action agreement. Rather than asking for the deal, you ask for specific features or choices implying that the prospect is buying. It could be argued that the tactic is borderline cheeky, but used in the right context this might be the nudge needed to close a deal.
  'Would you like us to start working on Wednesday or Thursday?'
  'Should we put you down for the Enterprise or Business solution?'

Sales processes are not always linear so let's look at other scenarios.

- **Early closure**

  Some prospects are in the market and ready to buy pro-vided they get the right solution. Your contact may already know your product and has made up its mind. Some of your inbound leads will fall into this category and such customers can be closed quickly. In these situations, there's no point in sticking to your standard script and walking your prospect through all of the stages of the standard sales process (e.g. presentations, demos, samples, visits, etc.), so make a step-change to closing-mode instead. Make hay while the sun shines!

- **Gone silent**

  There are situations where all objections have been deftly handled, the product is a good fit for the buyer and you've established a good rapport with the prospect, but suddenly all momentum is lost and so is the deal.

  There are a few rescue techniques you can deploy. For example, you could improve the deal for the buyer, but under the condition of meeting a deadline: 'I can give you another 3% for the first six months if you sign the contract by Friday.' 'I'd need your confirmation by Friday so that the engineers can commence work on the 1st August.' The tactic is not dissimilar to the closing techniques mentioned earlier. However, in this case you're trying to reactivate a customer that has gone silent. It really is a last roll of the dice to try and force a decision from your customer.

Closing deals should ideally fall into place and not have to be forced. If you've worked with the prospect, showcased the product, answered all questions and handled all objections the next logical step is to ask for the business. Closing a deal is about understanding your customer, finding the right message and delivering it with style to get the customer to sign on the dotted line.

The case study below is a prime example showing how the right strategy can help you close deals quickly.

....

Case Study: Winning and Retaining Business

Roll back time to the mid- 2000s when e-commerce turned into a mass market and online retailers started to send out millions of parcels each year to their customers.

For many decades, companies had been selling advertising space in catalogues and parcel deliveries. The rise of e-commerce and the subsequent growth of parcel deliveries gave inserting promotional material into packages, a much bigger platform than before.

Around this time, one of the biggest retailers in Europe decided to open their deliveries to advertisers. The sale of these parcel inserts was managed by an agency that had already been working with the retailer on other projects. But for this agency, the parcel-inserts were only a side job and they weren't eager to spend much time on it. They were passive and only handled incoming enquiries.

This opened a gap for Alex and his company. Alex had been in the insert-selling business for many years and knew the industry inside out. He had one massive insert contract with a publisher which was the main revenue stream for the small media agency he worked for. Because of this high-profile reference customer, he managed to get an entrance with the retailer. Nobody at the retailer was particularly keen to have two agencies working on selling inserts, but they agreed on a six-month test in which Alex could prove his worth. Mainly because they had unsold inventory and thought it would be little risk for them.

Alex knew instantly that he could turn this into a significant business for him. Within six months, he quadrupled insert sales. Why? Firstly, unlike the other agency he didn't just wait for enquiries, he went out and actively sold the inserts. But he didn't just do that, he also looked at the type of advertisers placing orders and then approached their competition. For example: 'Your competitor, bank XYZ, is inserting now in this online retailer's deliveries, why don't you? It's working for them, why shouldn't it work for you?'

He built his entire leads list by looking at the existing advertisers and would then call their competition. It worked phenomenally well for him. He not only won the account of the retailer exclusively after the six months, but he's retained it since and added new customers. When asked about his success factors he gave me the following answer, 'Always call on the senior management level. [In his industry that's normally the marketing director.] In fact senior people are very easy to deal with. They just want to know three things: 1) How much does it cost? 2) How will I earn a return on their investment? 3) How long does it take me to earn a return?'

He knows that if he follows this structure he'll get their attention and he often gets their business too. Why is calling on senior management different to calling on more junior employees? He says, junior staff tend to be more worried about how much work it means for them, whilst senior managers are concerned about how they can drive the business forward.

Looking at results

Your pipeline is not only about managing the sales process, but also about reviewing the results. This section is about taking stock and reviewing the performance.

Deals won

Deals won is obviously the most prominent assessment of sales performance. In Figures 13, 14, 15, 16 and 17, you will find a couple of classic graphs portraying deals won against the respective targets. All numbers are random so don't compare them against each other, but just reflect on the different ways sales performance can be presented.

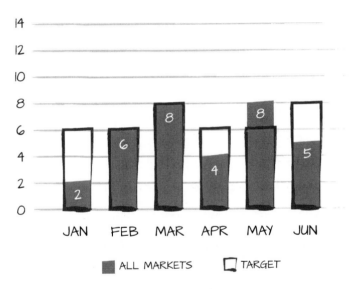

Figure 13: Deal performance by month

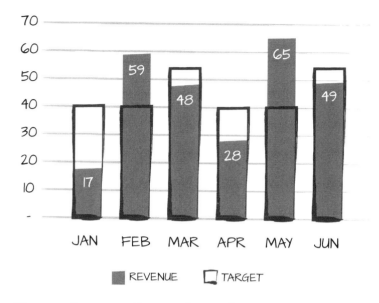

Figure 14: Revenue performance by month

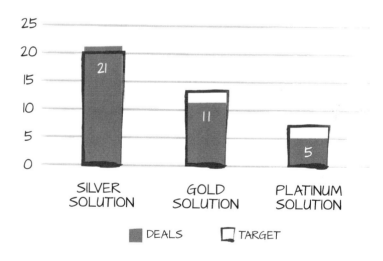

Figure 15: Deal performance by product

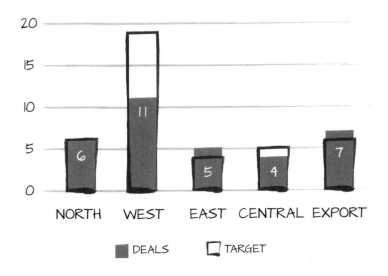

Figure 16: Deal performance by territory

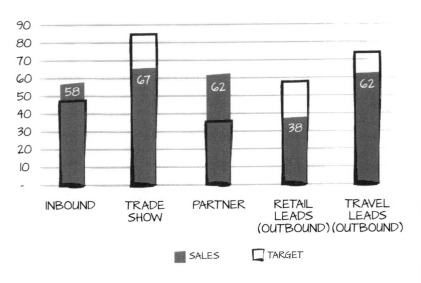

Figure 17: Revenue by lead source

Driving Sales Results

Deals lost

The flipside of winning deals is losing them, as you can see in Figure 18. There is value in looking at your lost deals, because they might reveal some insights as to how you can improve your work. If you're losing deals in specific product lines or in certain territories you might want to analyse why that is. Chances are you already know the answers but aggregated data can be more powerful than anecdotal evidence.

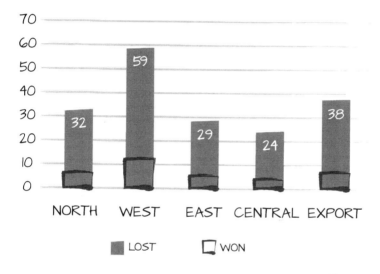

Figure 18: Opportunities lost by territory

Stage duration

Stage duration is the average number of days an opportunity spends in each stage. For most sales professionals, the longest duration is normally in the early stages, which gradually shortens towards the late stages. This type of sales cycle is illustrated in Figure 19.

Why longer in the early stages? Early stage opportunities are usually the biggest in numbers and the least advanced in the discussions. It's quite likely that you'll figure out in this stage that there's no progress or any chance of winning a deal which results in a lost opportunity. Before you give up, you might try a few angles, but if progress isn't achieved they'll be closed eventually. The process takes a while and that's mostly the reason why earlier stages have a longer sales cycle.

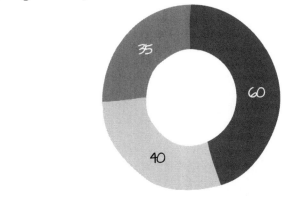

■ EARLY STAGE   ADVANCED STAGE   ■ LATE STAGE

Figure 19: Average stage duration in days

Figure 20 compares last year's sales cycle with the current year. This can be interesting to compare, particularly if there's a significant difference.

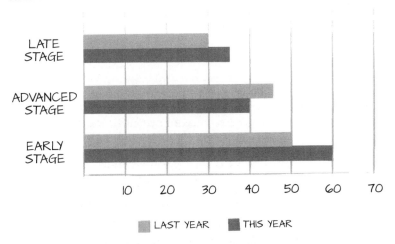

■ LAST YEAR   ■ THIS YEAR

Figure 20: Average stage duration in days vs last year

Driving Sales Results

Pipeline reviews are a classic exercise most sales teams do on a regular (weekly) basis. I haven't spoken about sales teams in this book, simply because it goes above and beyond the scope of this book, but below is a little case study about how difficult it can be to develop a team from scratch.

....

Case Study: Building A Sales Team

A small software-as-a-service start-up, was founded about a year ago. Of the two founders, one has a technical background and the other commercial. Their first 'friendly' deals were closed a couple of months ago through referrals and introductions from their wider network. In order to ramp up sales, they hired two junior employees with some sales experience. Nobody else in the company had worked in sales beforehand. The founders hoped that the new hires would just 'get on with it'.

They gave it their best shot, but in the absence of a sales method and combined with a lack of sales-skills and confidence, they made very little progress. Deals were coming in sparingly, if they came in at all. The situation was bleak and the start-up got under pressure to deliver. Eventually, the founders realised that urgent action was required. They found somebody who had built a sales team before to mentor the young duo. Performance started to improve and gradually, the two new hires started to bring in deals. They introduced procedures like recording all activities in a sales CRM, weekly pipeline reviews, a commission structure and on-the-job training with a sales coach.

Building a new sales function in a small company isn't easy and the start is often the most difficult phase. The first option is to go for an experienced sales professional with a track record, ideally in the industry. But they can be expensive and having had success somewhere else doesn't necessarily mean success in a new place. If the sales cycle of the product is long, you'd be paying a high salary for many months before you got to see the first results. Most small companies can't afford that.

Alternatively, you could hire young, hungry talent who is up for the challenge. There's a school of thought that you should hire not one sales professional, but two instead. The recommendation is that you let them lose on the market and see what happens. The bet is that at least one of the two will figure out how to make it work and that you can then hire more of the same profile. If you hired only one, so goes the argument, you'll never know whether the person's any good because you have no real reference for comparison.

Whichever option, developing a sales function from a standing start isn't easy. Making the right hiring decisions is always important but even more so when you're trying to build a team.

Conclusions

Managing the pipeline means managing the big picture (aggregate numbers) as well as the individual opportunities. Most sales teams tend to have a weekly pipeline review not only to report on the status of your projects, but also to keep in tune with each other and the rest of the business. Colleagues can rightfully make a realistic assessment of each other's sales performance, even if that can be uncomfortable at times as all eyes are on the dealmaker! In that sense, selling is a bit like motor racing. You can't win without your team, but when you're racing you'll be measured by your results as an individual. Managing your ability to perform is as important as managing the pipeline. Next, we look at deconstructing sales performance.

CHAPTER 5

Performance

Analysing the state of deals in your pipeline is one thing, but analysing your personal deal performance is an entirely different matter. It is much harder to be self-critical and sit in judgement on yourself. But it is something that has to be done. Being reflective and understanding what 'happened with this deal' is critically important because it's the basis for improvement.

When you look at the deals that you won and those you lost, what exactly is it that made the difference? Was it the product? The price? Or did you make a smart move in the negotiation process that sealed the deal?

Can you always be certain why you won or lost a deal? Maybe not, but later in this chapter you'll learn about a proven way that will improve your performance. First, however, let's look at an example that illustrates the difficulty of assessing sales performance.

John, a sales professional, has just received a call from Peter, a buyer at Amatrading. This is one of John's biggest opportunities in his pipeline. He's spent over eight months working on this deal, but his first contact, a cold-call, actually goes back three years.

John: Hi Peter, how are you? I've been waiting for your call.

Buyer: Hi John, I'm well, how about yourself?

John: It depends on your feedback on the proposal. You know how much this deal would mean to me and the firm.

Buyer: Sure. You know John, I've personally been an advocate of your product and I have observed you guys going from strength to strength over the past few years. That said, I owe you open and honest feedback so I won't be beating around the bush. The management board has decided to stay with Solutiontech (John's competition) and signed a deal with them for another three years earlier today.

I'm sure this must be disappointing for you, but you knew that Solutiontech as the incumbent would be a strong competitor in this tender process.

Whilst your offer was compelling, the board felt it was too risky to change suppliers at such a critical period for our company. We've had our ups and downs with Solutiontech in recent years, but overall they have been a reliable partner. Honouring a loyal supplier relationship means a lot to our senior guys. I can imagine that you must be very disappointed, but I can assure you that everybody here was impressed with what you've shown and the board asked me to personally thank you for all your efforts.

After a few more awkward minutes of conversation with John trying to discover if the deal was lost for good the call was over. Amatrading had signed with someone else.

John had been dreading *this* call for weeks. In the back of his mind, he had always known that it was a close race between him and Solutiontech, but he had invested so much effort in this deal, he couldn't bear to think about how he'd feel if he lost it. To start with, he had established the contact with Amatrading a few years back, which was an achievement in itself because colleagues who had tried before had failed. Since then he had built a great rapport with Peter, the buyer, but he also knew that a

Driving Sales Results

deal of such magnitude would always involve the senior brass at Amatrading so there was no way Peter could make the decision on his own.

Closing this deal, one of the biggest deals John had ever worked on, would have propelled him to rock star status in his company. Throughout the entire time he had worked on it, his CEO had closely followed John's progress. He doesn't normally get that level of attention from senior management. John reports to Nathan, the sales director, who, as you would expect, had also been heavily involved in the process.

Nathan can at times be like a bull in a China shop and during the negotiations he had rubbed up a few of Amatrading's senior staff the wrong way. Nevertheless, he had been a great ally to John when he had to negotiate the details of the offer (mainly pricing) with his CFO and the product delivery with his technical director. Without Nathan's help, the CFO would have stipulated terms which would have made it highly unlikely for Amatrading to even consider their offer in the first place. The CFO had been understandably concerned about how this deal would affect the overall profitability of the firm. John was never quite sure how aggressive the competition would structure their offer, so he just pushed for the lowest price possible.

Another thing that had made John uneasy was the lack of senior involvement in this deal. Whilst he had established a great relationship with Peter, Amatrading's buyer, John's CEO and other senior executives had had no contact with their counterparts at Amatrading. The old sales guard at Solutiontech, on the other hand, was known to have excellent relationships with the decision makers at Amatrading, some of them going back twenty years. John had felt this was an issue, but he couldn't really come up with a strategy to address it and frankly had questioned if it was even his responsibility to do so.

John had to admit that the sales team at Solutiontech were quite clever in picking holes in his product offering. He could tell by the way Amatrading's management asked him questions during his final presentation that those questions had been 'seeded' by Solutiontech in their final presentation. Could John have done more in his preparation to likewise pick holes in Solutiontech's offering? Possibly, but what about the marketing support that the sales team at Solutiontech gets? Plus, their sales director is a seasoned professional, a shrewd character who has built a great reputation in the industry. If anyone knew how to win over Amatrading's senior managers, it would be him.

Performance attribution

Question: Did the case study and all the ruminating about 'who did what' sound confusing and irritating? In general, the more complex the deal, the more difficult it is to assess when and why a deal is lost or won. Does it matter anyway? It matters because if you want to win such a deal next time, you need to understand why it failed this time. Generally, there will be two factors at play — the ones within your control and the ones outside of your control. When you're selling you're responsible for many things, but not for everything. Let's look first at the external factors.

External factors for losing the deal

Outside John's control:
Solutiontech was the *incumbent* company, which gave them an invaluable head start as they knew exactly how everything worked at Amatrading. With this information they could tailor their pitch much better than an outsider like John could.

Counter argument:
It could be argued that if there had been issues between Amatrading and Solutiontech during the previous contract term (Peter

alluded to 'ups and downs'), this wasn't necessarily an advantage. In other words, Amatrading would know the difference between what Solutiontech said they'd do in a sales pitch and their ability to deliver.

Outside John's control:
Solutiontech had long-standing personal relationships with Amatrading's senior team. Due to their ties, Amatrading's senior managers would have been personally inclined to hand the deal to Solutiontech.

Counter argument:
That's assuming that the personal relationship made a material difference in the decision-making process. Not every stakeholder will have had ties to Solutiontech. Even if some Amatrading managers did have personal ties they also had an overriding responsibility to *do the right thing* and avoid putting those ties ahead of the company interests.

Outside John's control:
There was so much at stake for Solutiontech that they would have offered almost any price to win the deal.

Counter argument:
Just like any other commercial company, Solutiontech has to make ends meet; they can't offer *any* price just to win the deal.

Outside John's control:
Solutiontech has an excellent sales director and Nathan wasn't experienced enough for this calibre of deal.

Counter argument:
There are other factors at play such as product, quality, service levels, pricing, trust, etc. Sales professionals can structure and

curate the conversation, but to a degree the facts speak for themselves e.g. price, product, quality, etc. In other words, sales can't mask every product offer deficiency.

Within John's responsibility

John's fault:
John had no counter strategy to address the lack of senior relationships between his company and Amatrading.

Counter argument:
If senior managers don't have a natural hustle to engage there's only so much John can do. Plus, in reality, how important are those relationships?

John's fault:
John appeared to be on the back foot in terms of setting the tone in the final presentation. The competition had most likely spoon-fed Amatrading with arguments exposing his company's weaknesses.

Counter argument:
Experienced senior managers are not easily fooled. Whilst Amatrading managers may have used some of Solutiontech's arguments to test John, they will have put this into the context of the overall offering. Although John obviously didn't engage in 'dirty-campaigning', every argument for John's solution will have caused them to compare it with Solutiontech's offering. It's unlikely that Solutiontech will have always come out on top.

John's fault:
Had John applied the BANT criteria rigorously in the early stages (qualification), he may have never pursued this opportunity. In hindsight, it appears that the company had no real intentions

Driving Sales Results

(need) to switch provider and Peter, the buyer, obviously didn't have the authority to close the deal.

Counter argument:
Amatrading appears to be a strategic account so it was right for John to engage and build a relationship. It's not been revealed how confident John was about this opportunity in the first place, but this attempt has possibly brought his company closer to winning the deal the next time round.

John's fault:
John appeared to be slightly lost in terms of Solutiontech's tactics and Amatrading's expectations. Perhaps he should have developed a stronger relationship with Peter, the buyer, which might have helped him sell this deal e.g. by asking, 'What do you think the senior management will expect to see from the winning party?'

Counter argument:
That's easier said than done. The competition will obviously hold their cards close to the chest and as will Amatrading.

This attribution exercise demonstrates how difficult it can be to pinpoint why you lose a deal and equally it can be just as challenging sometimes to understand why you've won a deal.

Despite the challenges in relation to attribution, reflecting on what went well and what didn't is a learning opportunity which creates awareness of all the factors that might have played a role in the customer's decision.

Finally, Dixon and Schertzer (2005) found that 'optimistic, self-efficacious salespeople are less likely to blame external forces' for their failures and 'they're more likely to work harder in response to their failures.' Optimism and self-efficacy will be discussed in more detail in the following chapter.

Foundations of sales performance

In a study in Canada (Barker, 1999), the styles of highly success-ful sales teams were compared with those of unsuccessful ones. It turned out that the successful teams *were more adaptive in their sales approach, providing better support to their customers*. It also revealed that they tried different selling styles and tailored their approach to the respective customer and the sales context. However, the study found no difference in terms of technical knowledge and selling capacity between the sales teams.

The author of the study described the style of the successful team as *behavioural orientation*. In plain English this means that when you work with the customer, you forget about the deal leader-board and your targets for a minute, and instead focus all of your atten-tion on meeting the needs of the customer. You need to grasp a full understanding of their situation, the problems they have and what you can do to help them find a solution. If you do this, your customer will experience a *tailored* response to their needs.

On the other end of the scale is *outcome orientation* which is about achieving control through a carrot and stick approach; in other words focusing on the actual output (leader board) and making managerial calls based on results. This could mean corrective action (closer scrutiny by a manager) for underperformance or rewards (e.g. spa weekend) for goal achievement.

Barker's study unambiguously concludes that behavioural orien-tation is a more successful way to practise sales. The not-so-subtle point in his study is a recommendation to focus on what is in your influence and not on what might be. It's within your influence to give your customer the best possible experience, to work on your sales skills and do this with great attitude. The deal target is the result of your work, but it can't be your guiding principle when working with individual customers. You can control your input, you can't control the output.

Driving Sales Results

In another study (Krishnan, Netemeyer, Boles, 2002), the researchers looked at the links between self-efficacy, effort and performance as shown in Figure 21. Self-efficacy is the extent to which you believe you are capable of accomplishing your (sales) goals. The study confirmed that there is, in fact, a strong correlation between self-efficacy, effort and performance. This is a very important dynamic for sales, because if you're confident in your capabilities to reach your targets, you'll put more effort into achieving them. You're creating a positive momentum by improving your selling abilities which, in turn, improves your actual performance.

This makes a lot of practical sense. If you want to close fifty deals in the next year and you believe this is doable and you believe in your abilities to achieve this, then you will be happy to expand all of the effort and energy required to get those fifty deals. On the other hand, if you're defeatist about your goal and your abilities, why even bother? The lack of self-efficacy and effort will consequently impact the result (performance).

The researchers also point out that training and learning leads to increased self-efficacy. So self-efficacy can actually be *learned* by working on your selling abilities.

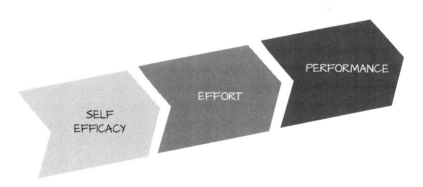

Figure 21: Sales performance: the link between self-efficacy, effort and performance. Source: Adapted from Krishnan, Netemeyer, Boles (2002)

At this stage, the main theme of this book ties in nicely with the findings of the research. If improving method, skills and attitude increases your ability to sell, it means you're growing your sales efficacy. In turn, sales efficacy leads to more effort and consequently a better performance. In short, if you're confident in your sales ability you'll be happy to make the extra effort to achieve your goals. What I've added to Figure 22 is some introspection which is the precondition for learning. It requires reflection about what works and what doesn't (attribution) to lay the foundation for improvement and learning.

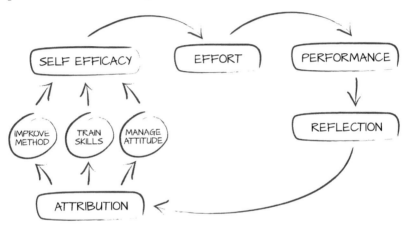

Figure 22: Method, Skills and Attitude leading to more sales success

Conclusions

Understanding what works and what doesn't work is the basis for improvement. The Amatrading case study shows that it's not always easy to pin down the root cause for winning or losing a deal. You can't control the output (leader board), but you can control the input. Controlling the input means you focus on what's there: the customer and your sales ability. The customer deserves the best possible experience. You deserve to be the best sales professional you can be. Bring the two together and you have a winning formula.

The next chapter will drill a bit deeper into how you can improve your ability to sell and deliver more winners. I will specifically focus on providing guidance on what aspects of sales you should concentrate on and how they link with each other.

CHAPTER 6

Your ability to sell

The three key aspects — method, skill and attitude — have to come together if you want to be successful. As we've discussed in the previous chapter, two out of three isn't good enough. If any of these are not up to scratch, sales performance will suffer. Good sales skills, but defeatist attitude? = not good. Great attitude, but no plan how to get leads and opportunities (method)? = unguided missile.

Within the subject of *skills*, the most important attribute is the ability to communicate. The wrong choice of words can completely destroy your pitch. I once worked with a junior sales professional who frequently used the phrase 'I suppose' or 'I guess' as gap-fillers during his pitch, blithely unaware of how unconvincing it sounded. Not only was he unaware of the effect, he simply had no idea that he was filling in the pauses in his speech with such wishy-washy words. In principle, there's no problem using the phrase 'I guess', but if you do it repeatedly, your audience will find your pitch unconvincing. It will be a major turn-off. So, skills and specifically communication skills will take up a significant part of this chapter.

While I've already covered *method* quite extensively in chapters three and four, with the main focus on getting leads and converting them into the pipeline, in this chapter there will be another practical view on sales method.

Finally, there will be a section on *attitude* and its proven links to performance. It discusses some exciting and powerful academic findings.

Being good at selling comes with a number of bonus side effects. When you're good at it — it's definitely more fun. When you sell with more confidence you're likely to get more satisfaction from your job. The end result should also be greater financial rewards for you.

Skills

Sales isn't a one dimensional profession, it requires a wide range of multidisciplinary skills. For example, being able to understand the fundamentals of a contract (legal), scheduling the implementation of a software solution (project management) or calculating a proposal (finance). The importance of these skills varies from industry to industry. For example, contract management can be very time essential in long-delivery, high-tech deals, but rather irrelevant in the world of media sales. As the star amongst all sales skills is communication and we'll look at that first.

Good communication skills

How we communicate matters. It matters in everything we do in life and it matters a great deal in sales. In fact, you could make the case that no-one is going to make it as a sales professional if they're not able to effectively communicate the benefits of the products they are offering to their client.

Effective listening

The first priority in the art of communicating, though, is not talking. It's listening. Silence is golden. Some sales professionals, especially junior execs, feel compelled to talk all the time because they think that's how you control a conversation.

But keeping quiet is never more important when you've revealed the price of your product. I learned from a sales veteran many years ago to remain silent at this critical juncture in the presentation. For example: 'The solution including the maintenance fees for the first year is £7,500'. [Silence]. Resist the temptation to fill the pause with an excuse such as, 'But maintenance is included so you don't have to worry about repairs'. And no further explanations like, 'If you paid within two weeks I could give you another 5 percent discount'. Maintain silence. Just pause and wait for a reaction. In my career I haven't had one occasion when I didn't get a reaction. Less is more when comes to talking.

Active listening requires your full attention, so in line with the earlier advice on cold-calling, don't let yourself be distracted by anything when you're dealing with a customer. When you're going into a meeting turn your phone to silent or, better still, turn it off. Don't use your laptop unless it's part of your presentation or absolutely essential. Focus on the conversation.

Show your customer that you're really listening and really paying attention by taking notes. After a long meeting it will be hard to recollect the entire conversion unless you have a good written record. And it is tremendously helpful to make note of key remarks made by the customer. Let's say, for instance, the customer says, 'We want to be number 1 in the flower category next year.' It's a powerful touch to play that back to them at your next meeting or on a presentation slide.

Finally, taking notes shows that you take the conversation serious-ly. It's a sign of respect. I always get nervous if I'm in the buyer's seat and in an hour-long meeting the sales professional doesn't take any notes. Wasn't anything said that was worth writing down?

A skill that's related to active listening is knowing how to 'read the room'. Great sales professionals are masters of picking up signals and hints from other people. They sense when someone's support-ive or signalling resistance. Remember John from the case study in the last chapter? Maybe a top sales professional would have picked up more signals and reacted differently? Of course, experienced buyers might be trying to mask their true intentions but, even so, you don't have to be an expert in body language to pick up some visual clues. Does your prospect look comfortable? Is he leaning forward? That's a sign of interest. Does he look bored? A big yawn would be a dead giveaway. Contradictions? Maybe the buyer is frowning whilst saying 'Looks nice'.

In this context, there are two books which I really enjoyed reading. The first one is by Joe Navarro and Marvin Karlins, *What Every BODY is Saying*, 2008. It's comes with many photos showing ex-amples of body language and Joe's background as an FBI agent which makes for interesting reading. It builds on sound academic research and is a good book if you're new to the topic.

The second book is *Peoplewatching: The Desmond Morris Guide to Body Language*, 2002. Morris is one of the pioneers of the field who started out as a zoologist. As the title indicates, Morris focuses on watching people's behaviour and the joy of observing is a key theme of his book.

The practical application of studying body languages to close sales is high, but Navarro and Karlins warn about jumping to conclu-sions too quickly. For example, just because somebody's got sweaty hands doesn't mean that this person is anxious. About 5% of the

Driving Sales Results

population have hyperhidrosis, a form of excessive sweating, so by just relying on one indicator your interpretation might be wrong.

What you should look for are changes in behaviour. For example, why somebody changes their body language when a certain topic comes up.

My personal take-away about body language is that observing supersedes interpretation. I'll never be a body-language expert, but I can be an eager observer and at the end of a customer meeting I try to put all elements together. What was said? How was the atmosphere? How was the body language? What group dynamics were at play?

By the way, watch your own body language. If you have an uptight negative posture, or you're fiddling with your hands, playing with your phone, checking your emails or, God forbid, even taking a call, the deal could be dead on arrival. Never forget that most people don't have to buy from you. Even if the product's good, there's always an alternative. An unpleasant sales professional can be reason enough for them to disengage.

Be mindful of making your prospect feel comfortable. Neuro Linguistic Programming (NLP) offers a technique called 'mirroring'. The technique is basically adjusting language, gestures and body language to the situation and specifically to your contact. For example, you'll find a different type of etiquette on a construction site than you would in a bank's head office. In both cases you should make an effort to fit in (to an extent) or, at minimum, not appear out of place. That's probably as much common sense as it is NLP. Whilst I found mirroring to be helpful in moderation, it goes without saying that you need to remain authentic, otherwise this approach might backfire on you. You could come across as an insincere actor.

Questioning

The best way to keep someone talking is by asking questions. Asking questions is the path to listening, which is the path to understanding your customer better.

Jobber and Lancaster have defined a few types of sales questions which go above and beyond the classic **open** questions, 'What would need to happen for you to sign the contract?' and **closed** questions like, 'If we gave you another 5 percent discount would you sign the contract?'

Type of question	Objective	Example
Tie-down question	Used for confirmation or to commit a prospect to a position.	You said you wanted to invest in a CRM tool, right?
Leading question Alternative question	Guides a prospect's thinking.	What do you think about the usefulness of CRM systems?
Alternative question	Used to elicit an answer by forcing selection from two or more alternatives.	Would you prefer to pay monthly or annually?
Statement/question	A statement is followed by a question, which forces the prospect to reflect upon the statement.	This solution has generated similar companies in your industry £500,000 incremental profit. Is this figure significant enough for your business?
Sharp-angle question	Used to commit a prospect to a position.	If I gave you a free upgrade to the platinum version, would you sign the contract this week?

Information-gathering questions	Used to gather facts.	What other marketing solutions have you tried in the past?
Opinion-gathering	Used to gather opinions or feelings.	What do you think will be the implications of the Smith Ltd bankruptcy on our industry?
Confirmation questions	Used either to elicit agreement or disagreement about a particular topic.	Is this a fair summary of our conversation?
Clarification questions	Reduces ambiguities and generalities	When you call our solution complex, what do you mean?
Inclusion questions	Present an issue for the prospect's consideration in a low-risk way.	Would you be interested to learn more about how 90% of our customers have reduced their downtime by 50% or more?
Counterbiasing	To obtain sensitive information by making a potentially embarrassing situation appear acceptable.	In our experience, most companies in our industry struggle to comply with all legal requirements. Have you ever found yourself in a similar situation?
Transitioning	Used to link the end of one phase to the next phase of the sales process.	Unless there's anything else you'd like to know about our payment terms, I'd like to move on to the order?

Reversing	Used to pass the responsibility back to the prospect by answering a question with a question.	Buyer: How long do you need to install the solution? Sales professional: When do you want the product?

Table 7: Types of sales questions. Source: adapted from Selling and Sales Management (Jobber, Lancaster 2009)

Negotiations

Negotiations are at the heart of many sales conversations and the stereotypical buyer-seller scenario is both parties arm-wrestling over prices. Jobber and Lancaster (2009) have a few ideas about who is in charge in a negotiation:

1. **The number of options available to each party**
   Due to the consolidation in retail over decades, a few supermarkets control the majority of the market. If you're a vendor to the retail industry, your mass market channels are extremely limited. It's a simplification of the situation, but basically you either dance to the retailer's tune or you're out. At the other end of the spectrum, if you're Wal-Mart and you're looking for a T-shirt supplier you're spoiled for choice. How hard or how easy negotiations are will depend on your position. In other words: are you Wal-Mart or are you the T-shirt vendor?

2. **The quantity and quality of information held by each party**
   'Knowledge is power.' (Machiavelli).
   The more you know about the other party and their circumstances, the better equipped you are to carve out a winning strategy.

3. **The need for recognition and satisfaction**
   Recognising needs and fulfilling them is closely tied to the

Driving Sales Results

topics of listening and asking questions. How else can you understand your prospect other than by listening, observing and asking questions? The better you understand your prospect, the better you'll be able to address the prospect's needs.

4. **The pressures on the parties involved**

There's an infamous story about an interview for a sales job where the interviewer asks the applicant to sell a water jug placed on the desk. The applicant goes to the bin in the corner of the room, lights a match and sets it on fire. He then asks the interviewer, 'How much for the jug'? It might be a slightly cheesy example, but it illustrates how quickly power can shift and obviously the more pressure a party is under, the weaker their bargaining power.

There seems to be a growing consensus in the business community that one-sided negotiations with one party winning and the other party losing is a bad result. The 'win-win' route is largely regarded as the better approach; however, in very competitive markets that's easier said than done. The fiercer the competition, the more commoditised your product, the harder your negotiation position is going to be.

No negotiation?

In tender-processes for large contracts, there is no real negotiation because buyers issue specifications detailing what they expect suppliers to deliver. Suppliers are then under pressure to hand in their very best offer as there might not be a second chance. If they're outbid in the first round, they're normally out of the process altogether. One tactic to circumvent losing out on the tender process is to engage the buyer at the earliest opportunity to influence the specification of the tender *before* it's issued. This makes sense because complex tender processes are also hard work for the buyers and they are often quite open to accepting help and guidance from sales professionals.

Negotiations and selling is as much an art as it is a science. Philip Delves Broughton in his book *Life's A Pitch: What the World's Best Sales People Can Teach Us All* (2012) illustrates it very nicely. He shares an anecdote from Larry Goodman, Head of Sales at CNN in the 1980s and 1990s. By 1987, the time when the following happened, the majority of the top advertising agencies in America were still not buying spots on Ted Turner's channels. Goodman took Turner to a sales meeting with an agency and it got off to a bad start. Some young executive started to talk down the cable networks, including Turner's CNN. Politely, but unmistakably. Turner initially listens '*and then he starts talking in this very low, slow voice: You know, every day, I wake up in my bed. I stretch. I get out of bed and walk to the window and look out over Atlanta. If it's sunny or raining, it doesn't really matter. It just feels good to be alive. I look back, and there's usually a beautiful woman in my bed. Sometimes two. Then I go to the kitchen and make myself a cup of coffee, pour a glass of orange juice. Then, you know what I do? I go to the bathroom and I take a fresh, original shit. Every morning. And you know what's in the bowl? That's what you're buying from the networks. Murder of the Week. What do I have that's fresh and original? Jacques Cousteau, National Geographic, twenty-four-hour news on CNN. Fresh and original? I beg to differ. What you're buying is a bunch of shit.*'

Two weeks later they received their first order from the agency.

Pfew...how's that for a negotiation strategy? It's quite a graphic example and Ted Turner definitely has a celebrity status that common sales professionals won't have. He does one thing though — he rebalances the power in the room. Rest assured that if Ted Turner had allowed the group to continue to attack his product, he wouldn't have sold anything. You don't need to be as impolite as Turner, but you're well entitled to stand your ground. If somebody tries to undermine you or your product, you must set the record straight. This concept is called framing. The general idea is that frames are set throughout conversations. For example, a buyer making you wait in the lobby for 30 minutes could very well be signalling that you're just not that important. Language, gestures, signs, etc. can all be aimed at undermining you. Oren Klaff has written an interesting book about this topic, called *Pitch Anything* (2012) which discusses different power scenarios and offers strategies to counter them. How much do you bare? How much is acceptable? There's a fine line between tactics and outright rudeness, but accepting targeted intrusions of your frame will put the buyer in charge of the conversation. Sometimes you need to put your foot down.

Presentations

Amongst the most important things about presentations is to know what you want. What does success at the end of the presentation look like? What audience is in the room? What questions are they likely to ask? How do you design the flow of the presentation? Working on a presentation is creative work and requires significant thought so I find that you need to start preparing at least a week in advance — even for a short presentation. You work your way gradually towards an engaging story. You don't need to spend a lot of time on it each day, but literally allowing yourself to sleep on it as it develops will increase the quality of the final presentation.

With regards to your message, be realistic about how much content you can cover in the time available. If you only have 30 minutes, you'll struggle to get more than five to six key messages across. It's better to deliver a few messages with maximum impact instead of trying to cram everything in.

Storytelling and influencing

Storytelling as a marketing and sales tool has become quite popular in recent years, even though it can be argued that sales people have been using stories to sell their products since the beginning of time. Storytelling for sales isn't about crafting a classic story through a hero or hero's journey, or other elements you'd find in a novel. It's about adding colour and emotion to your sales pitch. In fact, you're selling yourself and your organisation, so the value of storytelling goes much further than just the selling of a product.

You may think storytelling is like vapourware. Well, think again. Why do people buy sunglasses for £140? You can get perfectly functional sunglasses for a fraction of the cost of designer glasses, but people want the association of the brand and the story behind it. They actually buy into a lifestyle and pay a premium for it. Using stories in a sales context works in a similar way. If you can create value above and beyond the sum of your product's parts, than surely you are worth more to the customer than just the production price of the product.

Obviously, stories can't turn a bad product into a great one, but they can deliver added value to your customers. Specifically, when you're in a consultative sales situation your customers expect more than a sales professional who shows up and does a demo. They want to understand how you operate and where you're coming from, not least because if this is a longer-term relationship, they need more context and background before they can make a decision.

When I was working in consumer goods I would always tell customers the story of how I got into the industry in the first place. Here's what I would say:

I didn't just stumble into my first consumer goods job at Mars, I desperately wanted it. From an early age I was fascinated how global consumer goods companies managed to sell their products all over the world. I would go into my local supermarket in a small alpine village and buy a Mars bar and think about how, at the other end of the world, somebody else could be buying the very same product. Quite possibly at the same time. When I applied for a job at Mars, I was everything but the ideal candidate. I was inexperienced, much younger and had fewer educational creden-tials than other applicants. But I must have made an impression on them and after an initial interview round, they put me through a full day's assessment for which I had prepared my own product creation (the job was for a product development role). When I think back, I feel nothing but embarrassed because my little chocolate bar was so naïve, but my passion sold it to them and they offered me the job. I still remember jumping up and down in joy when they called me to say that I had passed the assessment and got the job.

You might think that's only an amusing story, you might think that storytelling doesn't work for you, but I can confidently tell you that everyone has a story to tell and stories matter to your customers, particularly when you're in a consultative sales role. Stories create connections and bonds.

When do you tell the story, though? You can't just blurt out stories randomly, can you? It's the art of sales to know when and how to say what, but there's almost always a time and a place for your story. Weave your personal story into the flow of the conversation and find an angle that gives you a hook-point to tell your contacts a little bit more about yourself. Credibility is a huge factor in de-cision-making and a good, genuine story about yourself can do wonders in this respect.

For both the product and the company stories you need to give your customers something that goes beyond reciting the press statement on your company website. Find something that adds meaning by making connections with your customers. In other words, why is your company (and product) relevant and important for them?

Stories are much more interesting than facts and figures. Nobody eagerly waits for a sales professional to come and read the specifi-cation sheet.

Chip and Dan Heath, in their book, 'Made to stick: Why some ideas take hold and others come unstuck', write about screenwriter Nora Ephron and her first day of journalism class. All of the students were assigned the task of writing the lede for a newspaper story of a high school faculty that was meant to travel to Sacramento for a colloquium in new teaching methods. Most students diligently recounted the facts and tried to condense them into a single sentence, like 'Governor Pat Brown, Margaret Mead, and Robert Maynard Hutchins will address the Beverly Hills High School....' (blah, blah, blah). The teacher collected all of the stories and then revealed what the lede should have been: *There will be no school next Thursday*.

The students missed the most intriguing fact of the story because it wasn't in the narrative they were presented. The lede could be found in what *wasn't happening* — school. Many of us as sales professionals are also often guilty of not working hard enough on the lede to our story. It's too easy to resort to the facts and figures instead of working out something more interesting and exciting for our audience.

Stories aren't just to showcase the product though; they're also important for yourself and your company. In particular, small business owners often have a strong conviction about their business and why they work in this field. Sharing your passion about your company and industry will make your pitch much more convincing. Company stories are an opportunity to give your organisation some personality. What's been an outstanding achievement of your company? How has it evolved? What have the challenges been and how have you overcome them?

Crafting a good story requires creativity, empathy and knowledge about your product, your industry and, most importantly, your customer. Great stories take the listener on a journey and they're tailored to capture the audience, so make sure you always have a few good anecdotes ready to relate. They certainly have to be backed up by actions, meaning your work needs to stand up to any claims in your stories, but they are more engaging than a 'technical' pitch. This is not to say that you should leave out facts and figures, but addressing the emotive side of your prospect will make the pitch 'stick'.

What else?

One of the best ways to work on your communication skills is to record yourself regularly. Whilst you can't record a call without permission, you can record your own voice with a digital voice recorder or a Smartphone when you're calling someone. When you rehearse for a presentation, record yourself and listen to it afterwards. Listen hard. More than once. I guarantee that every time you do this you'll find something to improve. It's simple and effective.

Repeating, summarising and paraphrasing, particularly towards the end of a conversation, is a good method to make sure everybody is on the same page. *'Can I just summarise what we talked about today?'* or *'We agreed on [....].'* If you're selling into other countries and cultures, it's all the more important to be clear and check that the other party has the same understanding at the end of a meeting as you do. This allows you to verify that what you heard is what the prospect meant and vice versa.

After a meeting or conversation you should always follow-up and send minutes containing the next steps that have been agreed. At the close of the meeting announce, *'After this meeting I'll summarise our conversation in an email. Please feel free to add and comment. In ten days, I'll then get back with a technical assessment and if you're happy, we can move ahead with an offer a few days later. The implementation could start as soon as you've signed the offer, so if everything goes smoothly, the product could be installed in about four weeks from now.'*

Finally, don't forget the humour. Most people like a laugh. A little bit of fun can break the ice and lighten the atmosphere. There's obviously a fine line between using humour effectively and going too far, but, in general, it's a great way to develop a rapport with your customers.

See how sales skills can be transferred from a corporate environment to a starting up your own company in the short case study below.

....

Case Study: Sales As A Transferable Skill

Peter has worked in sales for two decades. In his day job, he sells manufacturing machines costing upwards of £1 million. Having worked in the printing industry motivated him to start his own print management side business. He acts as a broker between customers and printing companies.

The advantage for his customers are lower purchasing prices and less hassle with the order process. Peter has excellent contacts in the printing industry and knows who to pick for what job. Because he manages to negotiate lower prices he can secure savings for his customers whilst retaining a margin for himself.

With regards to generating customers, Peter has a very simple strategy. He targets small to medium sized businesses and organisations in his region. He builds his leads list by looking at the Yellow Pages, internet search engines and trade organisations. Sometimes he runs a little direct mail or email campaign to generate a few inbound leads.

Once a week he sets an afternoon aside (remember, he's doing this part-time) and blitzes through 20 to 30 leads (mainly calls) in one hour. He tries to speak to the owner or the managing director, but if he can't get through, he asks for the email address and follows-up with a short, concise and personal email introducing his service. Within a few months he managed to get the monthly revenues up to £10,000 — not bad for a couple of hours of work each week.

Peter is generating value by connecting two parties: buyers (e.g. a tourist board) and sellers (a printing company). With practically no investment, he's built himself a little company. He's got years of experience in sales and lives by two credos. The first one is, 'You have to trust your process.' In his day job (selling machinery), the sales cycles are anywhere from six months upwards so he has to trust that his actions will lead to success. Peter's second credo is, 'If a buyer views you as a sales person, you have already lost.' Nobody wants to buy from product pushers. Both credos have served him well as he's very successful in what he's doing. Selling is easy when you know what you're doing.

Commercial skills

Sales teams are often at the forefront of any company's commercial activities as they have access to many different aspects of business. They deal with customers, competitors, their own finance and marketing team (where applicable) and, therefore, have a very comprehensive view of the environment around them. Hence, commercial skills are an important part of all sales skills.

Product and market expertise

If you take expert- or solution-selling seriously, then you have to have a solid knowledge about your industry. There's no excuse. The only reason for not doing so is a lack of willingness. Don't fall into the trap where your customer knows more about your product than you do. What could be worse than that?

Demonstrating a business case

Sometimes a sale can be complex, particularly when you're entering new territory. For example when you're introducing a new product, or setting up a new type of partnership, or entering a new market, or establishing a new key account with different requirements. In these situations, a deal might look more like a project than a sale, so it might be necessary to present an entire business case demonstrating the viability of your offering. You might need to document more research than usual, provide assumptions about how the business will be involved, and assess implications on the wider business, ultimately all leading to a recommendation (and a sale). Perhaps the terminology 'business case might sound a bit grand, but it's really nothing more than putting a sound argument together.

Calculations

You don't have to be a maths whizz to be a successful sales professional, but being solid in doing basic calculations is a must. In fact, financials are almost always used as a sales argument. Two of the most popular ones are return-on-investment (ROI) and break-even analysis, which I will now discuss.

Return on Investment

Megan advertises her online store on a search engine. For every visitor clicking on her ad, she pays a fee to the search engine provider. About one in ten visitors ends up buying. She pays £1 per visitor, so ten visitors cost her £10. One in every ten ends up buying, so she needs to spend £10 to get one customer. That's her cost-per-acquisition (also often called CPA). Her average order value of a single customer is around £30 with a contribution margin of 40% (= £12).

Investment cost: £10
Order Value: £30
Contribution margin (40%): £12
ROI (return-on-investment): $(12/10) - 1 = 20\%$

The ROI is 20% so that makes it worth her spending money on the search engine.

Break-Even Point

Tom sells ice cream machines to coffee shops and kiosks. They cost £2,000 each and tend to generate a contribution margin of about £1 from each portion sold. For this to become a cash-profitable operation, the fixed costs (£2,000 cost of the machine) have to be covered first. The break-even point marks the very moment when the cost of £2,000 has been covered by the margin made from all ice cream sales.

Fixed cost: £2,000
Contribution margin per portion sold: £1
(The contribution margin is the sales price (excluding tax) minus the cost of the product (variable cost))
Break-even: 2,000/1= 2,000 portion

Standard calculations

Calculating the (value added) tax:
Tax goes to the taxman so it needs to be excluded if you want to look at net sales. B2B prices are often quoted net and the VAT is then *added* on the invoice. Make sure your customer understands your offer — whether VAT is included or not. VAT is, of course, country and product specific.

Calculating the net price:
Gross selling price including VAT: £135
VAT: 20%
Net selling price (excluding VAT): 135/1.20 = **112.5** (= £112.5)

Calculating a discount:
Selling price: £100
Discount: 20%
Reduced selling price: 100*(1-20%) = **80** (= £80)

Calculating the contribution margin:
Selling price excluding VAT: £80
Variable costs: £40
Contribution margin: (80-40)/80*100 = **50%**
Absolute contribution margin: £80-£40 = **£40**

Mark-up:
Unlike the contribution margin, the mark-up is calculated by using the cost price as the denominator. The mark-up is therefore twice the contribution margin.
Selling price: £80
Variable costs: £40
Mark-up: 80/40*100-100 = **100%**

Contracts

Most sales jobs involve some level of contract management. Even if contract drafting needs to be handled by a professional, having some basic understanding about how a contract looks and being able to read one is a useful skill. Eventually, a lawyer can be called in to help put the final document together, but they'll need guidance on how to structure the deal. Misunderstandings between you and the lawyer can cost you dearly.

Productivity

Managing your time and working effectively are two key aspects of sales. It could be argued that ultimately you're selling your time, so the more productive you are the higher your return on selling.

Goal setting

The reason why goal setting is included in this book is because it's so tightly knit to the DNA of sales. Many sales teams are single-mindedly focused on goals, because they understand the impact of it on their performance. It's also often reflected in the culture and the

Driving Sales Results

symbolism of sales teams (e.g. leader-board, status perks like a trip to Las Vegas).

Edwin A. Locke and Gary P. Latham (2002) have written an excellent article, *Building a Practically Useful Theory of Goal Setting and Task Motivation*, with lots of useful foundations for sales professionals.

Some of their key findings are:

1. **Goals work much better than just aiming to do your best**
   The problem with 'doing your best' is that it's incredibly vague.
   In the absence of a reference point (a specific goal) you end up with a wide range of acceptable performance levels. Retrospectively, you can quite easily convince yourself that you did your best when you didn't.

2. **The higher and the more difficult the goals, the higher the effort and performance**
   In other words, the higher you reach, the further you'll go. They found that performance only levels off or even decreases when the limits of individual ability are reached or when the commitment lapses.
   For example, if you've never played tennis and your goal is to beat a friend who's a very good player, you're likely to be frustrated after the match. It might actually be counterproductive to you *learning* how to play tennis. If you made tennis a *learning goal* instead of a *performance goal*, then hitting the ball correctly is more important than beating your friend. By steadily improving your skill set you may get to a level where you can challenge your friend. That would be the stage where you can take on a performance goal such as beating your friend in a match or, at least, winning a set.

In a field where you already have the skills and the experience, performance goals do make a lot of sense. For example, if you've been closing 10 deals each quarter, could you close 15? Maybe that's ambitious, but it's not really a matter of ability because if you *can* close 10 deals a quarter you can also close 15 with a push.

3. Goals have to be specific AND ambitious

Goals have to be specific and ambitious. For example, 'following up with every prospect enquiry' is specific. 'Following up with every customer enquiry within 12 hours' is specific and ambitious.

There are more reasons why goal setting works. First, goals are *directive* and therefore help you to focus whilst *avoiding* things that may distract you. Second, they are *energising*, motivating most people to rise to a challenge. Finally, goals also affect *persistence* and *action*, because if you've committed to something you tend to keep going.

There are a few things that influence goals:

- **Commitment**

  If there's a strong goal commitment, then you're more likely to achieve it. Monetary rewards can increase the commitment and therefore have a positive effect on reaching targets, hence the popularity of sales commissions. There is a caveat however: If the reward is only given upon 100 percent achievement of a goal, people tend to stop pursuing it when they realise they won't make it. For example, if you get a £5,000 bonus for closing 15 deals and you realise one month ahead of the deadline that you won't make it, there's a good chance that you will slow down or move your late stage opportunities into the next sales quarter. Keep this in mind when you are assigning a performance-related commission.

- **Importance**
  The more important a goal is to you, the higher your commitment will be. One tactic to increase importance is by inflicting social pressure on yourself, by making your goal public, e.g. publishing 'I'll run a marathon next year' on social media.

- **Self-efficacy**
  We covered the topic of self-efficacy quite extensively in Chapter 5 *Performance*. The essence was that higher levels of self-efficacy are reached by improving one's sales skills. Unsurprisingly, the higher the self-efficacy the higher the goal commitment because the trust in your abilities translates into higher confidence and therefore increases your goal commitment.

- **Feedback**
  Goal feedback is reasonably unambiguous in sales, as there is very little room for interpretation about the actual performance — a deal closed is a deal closed and targets hit are targets hit. This direct relationship between performance and goal in sales is also a catalyst to force 'corrective action' when you're off target. In other words, if you're behind, you'll be expected (by yourself and your team) to double down.

- **Task complexity**
  Task complexity can be detrimental to goal achievement if it requires you to learn new abilities. For example, take the challenge of learning to play tennis that I quoted earlier. It's hard to have a performance goal (win a match) when you haven't developed the skills and the experience yet (playing tennis). In a sales context that means that either you're junior and haven't mastered the sales skills yet, or you're working on a new product and the sales process hasn't been fully figured out.

There's plenty of evidence that goals work in a sales environment. Established sales teams normally use the budget planning process to define goals for the upcoming period. With fewer resources available, smaller companies tend to be less diligent, but goal setting doesn't have to be a complex undertaking. Top line numbers like lead generation, lead qualification, and deal- and sales-targets will provide baseline-goals that can be reviewed on a regular basis.

Other productivity considerations

The waking hours of your day is all the time you've got. How you spend those hours is determined by the choices you make. Hence, decision making is closely intertwined with time management. The better your decisions on topics such as *What is important today?* or *Which activities will help me to achieve my goals in three months?* the more effective you'll be.

Time management is important and keeping a calendar is particularly useful. Whenever you arrange a meeting, put it into your calendar so that the time is blocked, but also send your contact an invitation and check if the invitation has been accepted. This reduces the risk of anyone, including you, missing the meeting. It's also good business practice to confirm the meeting with your contact the day before or even earlier if you have to travel a long distance. The last thing you need is to arrive at the agreed location only to find that your contact isn't there because they have forgotten the meeting.

Related to this is a Harvard Business Review (HBR) article from Adamson, Dixon, and Toman (2013) who suggest using verifiers instead of just scheduling or completing tasks. For example, a task is 'meeting the customer for the product demo on 20 August at 2 p.m.'. A *verifier* is, 'the customer has given notice to his current supplier and they're actively looking for a new solution to be implemented by 30 January of next year'. Therefore, instead of just scheduling a follow-up with your customer, it's more useful to get a commitment to move the opportunity to the next stage. If you struggle to get the commitment, it's quite possibly a sign that there are challenges with this deal.

In general, technology is becoming more and more prevalent in selling. It pays off to be reasonably proficient in the use of spreadsheets in order to create forecasts, customer offers, price calculations, performance analysis and graphs for presentations.

Having the best sales skills in the world is rather useless, however, if you're not good in the execution. For instance, if you promise your prospect that you'll send a proposal in three days you have do exactly that. If for some reason you can't meet your commitment, let your customer know before the deadline passes (but don't make it a habit). Anecdotal evidence suggests that top sales professionals are masters in following up.

Project management skills are helpful when your product is reasonably complex and requires some level of implementation/installation — the deployment of a new software solution, for example. Whilst you don't have to be a fully-fledged project manager, being able to coordinate all aspects of a task is a reasonable expectation.

Finally, what's the best way to improve those all-important skills? You need to become a 'Learning Practitioner', somebody who *learns* and *applies* what they have learned on an ongoing basis.

That's because an estimated 87 percent of new skills learned are lost within a month unless they are reinforced, according to a behavioural training study by Sullivan. Perhaps you've attended a training course which you found useful, but couldn't remember the first thing about it a few months later? The acquisition of sales skills needs to be an ongoing process; part of it being training on the job, part of it coming from self-development (e.g. literature) and part from training programmes. If you're lucky, you will have found yourself a sales mentor or a sales manager who can help you in this process.

Method

When it comes to the sales method, there are two interesting developments. Large companies with optimised sales processes seem to increasingly struggle by having set procedures in place — particularly if they are operating in a fluid market. In technology, for example, most companies have to regularly reinvent themselves. There aren't many industries left where change isn't the new norm. Hence they look for new ways to give their sales reps more liberty in how they do their job whilst retaining some level of management control.

On the other hand, there is a new wave of small businesses and entrepreneurs who are nothing short of agile, but who are often untrained in sales. Whilst they are very quick and responsive to opportunities, they often lack a structured sales process. If these small businesses are fast enough to crack the sales code, then it's just another obstacle that they have overcome on the road to success. If they don't master the art of sales, the resultant lack of sales is often lethal.

We have already discussed the *sales funnel* in Chapter 3 *Getting started with leads*, which covers the notion that you have to filter a large number of leads through the funnel in order to achieve a smaller of number deals. Alongside the sales funnel sits the *sales cycle* which describes each individual sales discussion, from the beginning of the conversation with the prospect right through to analysing customer needs, demonstrating the solution, proposing an offer, dealing with any objections and eventually closing (or losing) a deal.

Whilst the sales funnel and the sales cycle both describe the same idea, however, the funnel includes *all* leads and opportunities whilst the sales cycle only focuses on the individual sales conversation as illustrated in Figure 23.

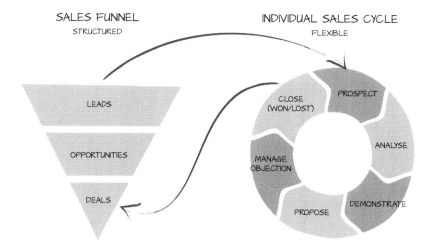

Figure 23: The Sales Pipeline and the Sales Cycle

If I had to assign a mindset to the sales funnel, it would be *structure* and *process*. For the sales cycle it would be *flexibility*. Are a structured process and flexibility mutually exclusive? No. In sales, there's a time and a place for both.

The structured process is important when you build and manage your sales funnel. For the funnel to be healthy, you need a steady stream of leads and plenty of activity in your pipeline to keep opportunities moving. In order to manage the funnel successfully you need to make sure the numbers come in, the quality checks are in place, and its state is monitored regularly.

In the sales cycle, on the other hand, flexibility is the watchword. Every conversation with a prospect or a customer is different, so it's pointless trying to fit everyone into the same mould. Being flexible is normally a strength of small companies because they're used to changing environments and the need to make things work, regardless of the circumstances.

Having a sales method is important, otherwise sales can become very random and unpredictable. If you want steady streams of new revenues from sales, you need to embrace a structured process. Read the case study below and see how a methodical test-and-learn approach eventually leads to sales results.

....

Case Study: Finding Innovative Ways To Reach The Customer

Danielle got into sales after university. She started working for a small upmarket portrait photography chain selling photo sessions. She did really well in this job and soon turned into the company's top performer. After a couple of successful years in the UK, she was sent to the US to ramp up their American business.

In the UK, the company had built their customer acquisition with mobile stands in shopping malls selling to passing shoppers. They had tried the same approach in the US, but with very little success. Firstly, shopping malls in the US were less interested in renting out space and when they managed to get space, they had low conversion rates. The model that worked so well in Europe, didn't quite cut it in the US. Danielle had to get creative and find new ways of generating business. One of those tests was selling photography sessions at art festivals. It turned out to be hugely successful. People interested in art, so says the hypothesis, have a natural interest in high-quality (portrait) photography. Danielle sold the actual photography session cheaply. Customers would only have to pay $50 for a studio session of up to 2 hours — much less than the actual cost of the studio and the photographer's time. The $50 for the session would have to be paid by the customer at the point of booking. The customer could then attend the session with their family and even get a free printed photo in a frame when they returned for the

Driving Sales Results

viewing in the studio. Whilst there, they would also be presented with other photo merchandise such as books, canvases and accessories. Whilst customers could in theory leave the studio with a printed photo in a frame and not pay anything (other than the initial $50), in reality many customers actually spent hundreds or even thousands of dollars on photo merchandise. Once they saw their photos on beautiful canvases, they couldn't resist.

Danielle's biggest success was setting up operations at fundraising events. The kind of event where, over dinner, a few items are auctioned off and participants pay for the dinner itself. In a two hour period such fundraiser events could easily generate up to 30 deals (bookings) with high quality customers. Not only was this a phenomenal number for two hours of work, fundraiser participants were affluent, high-quality customers who would spend up to ten times above the average customer. Danielle agreed with the fundraising-organiser that they could keep all of the $50 booking fee she would charge on that evening. On top of it, she would also provide a photographer to the event who took some photos during the evening and provided guests with a few free prints on their way home.

Some of these evenings could generate as much as $25,000 in business, in other words customers buying photo merchandise. It is no wonder the company asked her to return to the UK and replicate the success of these new initiatives which she did.

This story is about being creative in finding new customers and about acknowledging that what might work in one country doesn't have to work in another one. Danielle understood both. She's now in a leadership position of a large sales driven company.

Attitude

Working in sales comes with a number of emotional and mental challenges some of which we have already discussed such as dealing with rejection, target pressure, pushback from customers and cold-calling anxiety. Sales is a customer-facing role, so for sales professionals there's nowhere to hide. Prospects and customers expect a top performance from sales professionals just as they would from an actor in a theatre regardless of what else is going in their lives. If you're not in a good frame of mind, most activities like prospecting, presenting, negotiating, networking, etc. will become very challenging.

Adding to this pressure is role ambiguity. For example:

- You're about to close a deal, but your production team tells you they don't have the capacity to fulfil the order.
- Your customer demands a marketing contribution, but your marketing team tells you their budget's tied up in campaigns.
- The finance director increases prices to improve profitability, but your customers threaten to leave you for the competition if the new prices are enforced.
- You have found that certain types of customers with insufficient IT resources have proven to be high maintenance and low-profit customers, but your company still wants you to continue closing deals in this segment.

These are just a few examples and, in all of these cases, there's a good reason for both arguments. Finance might be concerned with profitability, but equally sales might be concerned about the customer relationship. Despite all the challenges, let's also not forget the positive side of sales: the buzz, the excitement and the satisfaction of closing deals.

When you're in sales, you are performing a role. In many ways like an actor because there's an element of showmanship. Actors, for example, train to 'get into character'; meaning they work on impersonating the behaviour of the character they're playing. It's the same in politics. I love the story that Bill Clinton, whenever he has to go on stage, allegedly says 'Show time!' to prepare himself mentally for the performance ahead. Selling requires a level of conviction simply because if you don't show a strong belief in your product how can you expect your prospect to believe in it? In this context, you may want to watch Amy Cuddy's TED Talk, *Your body language shapes who you are* (2012). One of her findings is that our bodies change our minds. Only a few minutes of certain poses can increase your testosterone and lower your cortisol. The increase in the former makes you more confident, the fall in the latter increases your stress resistance. Power-pose yourself to confidence. Fake it till you become it.

Hopefully most of the time you'll find selling quite easy, but occasionally when the going gets tough you may have to say to yourself, 'Show time!' and perform a few power-poses, before you go into a meeting or on a call with a prospect.

One thing is certain — a miserable and unconvincing performance isn't selling. So being in sales on a good day is easy, but how you deal with yourself when you're having a bad day can make all the difference.

In 1985, Marty Seligman, one of the leading psychologists of our time, conducted a large study with the insurance company MetLife. He wanted to find out whether the optimism levels of new sales recruits made a difference to their performance. The findings are mind-boggling. In the first year, optimists outsold pessimists by 8 percent. So far so good, but in the following year, they outsold them by a staggering 31 percent! Even more interestingly, one group called 'special force', which was made up of applicants who had *failed* the MetLife's general career test but scored in the top half in Seligman's optimism test, outsold pessimists by 21 percent in the first year and by 57 percent in the second year! In short: Optimists sell!

So where does this difference come from? The answer lies probably in the stronger persistence of optimists. Failure, rejection and setbacks are inevitable in sales. If you're a pessimist, this will fuel and confirm your negative assumptions and potentially send you on a downward spiral. If you're an optimist, you'll regard setbacks as a temporary nuisance. Can you train to be an optimist? Well, Seligman points out that your explanatory style is decisive in how you assess situations. If your description of bad events is *permanent*, *pervasive* and *personal*, then you're up for a pessimistic rollercoaster.

Look at the comparison below. You will find the pessimistic explanatory style in the left column and an optimistic explanatory style in the right column. Optimistic doesn't mean that you twist every setback into a positive statement as you can see in table 8, it's just handling it in a less negative way.

Pessimistic explanatory style	Optimistic explanatory style
Permanence	Temporary
Cold calls **never** work.	The **last** cold call failed.
Pervasiveness	Specific
Everyone hates cold calls.	I called them at an inconvenient **time** and our **product** really wasn't for them, so the call ended quickly.
Personal	External
I'm bad at selling.	**It** wasn't meant to be last week.

Table 8: Explanatory styles

Driving Sales Results

Do any of the left hand quotes sound familiar to you? Most of us are guilty of indulging in doom and gloom scenarios from time to time. More often than not, things aren't anywhere near as bad as we like to believe they are.

Watch out for your explanatory style and if you're going through a tough period, treat yourself to a more upbeat explanation of recent events and remember the performance statistics mentioned above. Seligman is quite clear that there's a positive side to pessimism and he found that (mild) pessimists do better than optimists in jobs which require a pronounced sense of reality. For example, nobody wants an overly optimistic Health & Safety officer. However, selling is without a shadow of a doubt a profession where optimists win.

In the context of how important attitude is in a sales job, the case study below shows how persistence pays off in the long term.

....

Case Study: Persistence

Henry sells accessories to the electronics industry. Whilst selling direct to the customer through their website, most of the items are sold through retailers and partners. Closing distribution deals isn't easy. Retailers and partners tend to be big companies so there are layers of management and they tend to operate much slower than small companies. Nevertheless, Henry has done well and he's built out distribution deals over the last few years. His product is competitive, but the competition sells decent products too. So how did Henry do it?

'Persistence is the key. In many cases we've been knocking on doors for years and years until something came from it. Large companies tend to be slow. We have closed a partnership deal with a large electronics manufacturer and they'll sell our accessories through a pre-installed app,

but getting to this point was a long journey. However, we never gave up and we impressed them with our flexibility. That often got us to a point, where these partners wanted to work with us. They almost wanted to give us a chance, even though we're an underdog for them. Our sales are small and we're still very much a start-up, but we didn't let that deter us.'

All of this leads us to the next and final chapter: an overall review of everything I've presented in Driving Sales Results. The last chapter of the book encapsulates my formula for a winning career in sales.

CHAPTER 7

Mastering sales

Can you ever fully master sales? Maybe not. Mastering sales is more like an ongoing journey than a final destination, but with a little effort you can certainly become extremely proficient and successful. So what's really important in this quest to master sales? Let's review what we've covered in the pages of this book.

In my view the five themes below have the biggest impact on your performance.

#1. Start with the customer

There's hardly any other job that gets you closer to the customer. However, keeping your focus on the customer isn't always easy. Pick a normal day in the office and add target pressure, demanding customers, rejection, organisational problems and the special flavour of the day, like 'margin alert', and chances are that your customer focus quickly fades.

So when you're pulled in every direction, try to reset your focus and ask yourself, *what's important for the customer?* All of the other office work is not irrelevant, of course, but if you're in sales you need to constantly remind yourself that the customer takes precedence over everything else. I appreciate that this is a statement of the obvious, but, at the same time, I know for a fact that many sales professionals are juggling so many other tasks that a *customer first* approach is often wishful thinking.

So where do you place that customer first focus? My focus in this book has primarily been on the strategies you need to deploy to win new business. But it's equally important to keep nurturing existing customers. It's nearly always cheaper to retain existing customers than find new ones, so don't let the relationship with them deteriorate while you are in hot pursuit of new ones.

Every customer is a great source of information and we discussed the importance of listening skills in Chapter 6, *Your ability to sell*. Listening is an acknowledgement that every customer is different, has individual goals, problems and issues. Listening to the customer and working with the customer will help you to better understand each customer's environment and make it a smoother journey for both parties.

This is not an over the top recommendation. In today's complex and noisy business environment, this customer mindset needs a little extra attention. To reiterate: I'm positive that many sales professionals are spending the majority of their time on activities far removed from the customer, being a bit customer obsessive will help bring allocation of time back into balance.

#2. Embrace the process

Many small businesses ignore the need for planning and are inclined to work off the cuff. I'm not finger-pointing because, as I've mentioned earlier, most small businesses often don't have the luxury of an expert in every field, so the person who handles sales often has to juggle many other tasks. The problem with a hands-off approach, however, is that the whole sales process becomes very murky and unmanaged. As a result, important tasks such as lead generation and lead qualification are often put on the back burner because there's no understanding of how many leads need to be worked to achieve actual sales targets. One way to circumvent this is by being diligent with your numbers. Do you know your stats? Do you know how many contacts you have to make in order to close one deal? What type of lead converts best and what type has the highest value?

Perhaps you're thinking that your operation is too small and that analytics aren't relevant to your business? You would be wrong. A quick, simple fact check can make a big difference: just a little record-keeping to track your leads run-rate (e.g. in the last quarter) compared with the number of deals you've closed (you'll probably know *that* number, for sure).

Thanks to technology, data is now more readily available than ever before. For example, fitness apps on smartphones produce a wealth of information. All you have to do is carry your smartphone with you when you're starting your exercise routine. It can actually be quite entertaining to compare yourself with peers (well, it can sometimes be depressing too).

Whilst CRM solutions are nowhere near as engaging as some consumer applications, most of them will give you solid insights about how you're performing, provided, of course, that you fed the system with data in the first place. The out-of-the-box reporting functionality is often good enough for most small businesses. Standard reports will work fine, especially as you're in sales, not data science. Having access to data also allows you to benchmark yourself with other sales professionals and, finally, data forms the basis for any credible sales plan.

Don't forget about your sales strategy. Strategy might be a grand word for what is, in fact, just clarity about your sales environment. Who are your target customers, how do you sell profitably and why would customers buy from you? If you lack clarity on any of these questions you could be actively selling, but failing to close deals. Put simply: you're spinning the wheel with no direction.

#3. Actions speak louder than words

When I first moved to the UK, I worked as a sales executive for Amazon's seller services team. There were about 15 of us in the team. My English skills were OK, but as a native German speaker who had never lived in an English-speaking country before I wasn't anywhere near as fluent as the locals. Part of my job involved dealing with German companies, but more than half of my deals were closed in the UK.

In my first quarter, I became the top-performing sales executive, despite my initial lack of product knowledge and my language deficiencies. Why? Because I hit the phone more often than anyone else. I felt handicapped due to my below par language skills. I often thought I could do so much more if only my English was more fluent. But that handicap only spurred me on to work harder. I was determined to make it work. It goes to show that with an ambitious goal and some determination you can go a long way in sales. I have seen that in other people, too, in opposite ways. I've seen very talented people perform very poorly and I've seen mediocre people do very well and in both cases it was all down to effort. It is a simplification, but valid to note, that talent combined with low effort equals poor results; mediocre skills and hard work equals better results.

Nothing beats picking up the phone and making calls, writing emails, researching the prospect and being valuable for the cus-

Driving Sales Results

tomer. You can only be valuable if you have context about your customer's challenges and you can only get context by doing your homework.

Sales is about going out there and finding new business with both existing and new clients. It is about turning rocks and finding opportunities. It's about pitching your heart out. You won't always be successful, but if you never try, you'll never know. As the saying goes, 'Actions speak louder than words.'

#4. Never stop learning

Writing about learning in this section is a bit like preaching to the converted. You've almost read to the end of this book so congratulations — you've already made an effort to develop yourself further in the field of sales. You don't need much convincing. But a good part of learning is reflecting on what you've learned to make sure it is embedded in your brain.

Learning happens in many ways, but for sales professionals in smaller companies or start-ups, it's likely to be learning on the job and self-directed learning. Having access to a sales manager or a HR department that manages learning for you is a less likely scenario. The good news is that some studies have shown that self-directed learning is highly effective (e.g. Boyer and Lambert: *Take the handcuffs off sales team development with self-directed learning*, 2008). Just because you're working on your own or in a small team doesn't mean you're disadvantaged in your learning opportunities.

In this context, I found another study highly interesting. Two scientists, Frayne and Geringer (2000), provided self-management training to sales professionals in areas such as self-assessment, goal-setting, self-monitoring, self-evaluation, and written contracts (as in a contract with yourself to pursue certain goals). In comparison with a control group which received no training, they made an average of 50 percent more calls, sold twice as many insurance policies and generated 150 percent (!) more in sales revenues. The sales professionals got help in order to help themselves and it worked exceptionally well.

It's not just the result of the training that's intriguing, it's also the topics covered. Self-assessment, self-monitoring, self-evaluation and so on are all areas of introspection and they have particular value for sales, because every deal — regardless of whether it is won or lost — is an opportunity to reflect. Every reflection can be a starting point for a learning exercise. If you felt that your last presentation could have been better, maybe you should consider brushing up on your storytelling and presentation skills?

Live to learn... well, actually sell, learn and sell some more.

#5. Don't lose your swagger

Confidence is attractive. Confidence sells. How do you achieve confidence in selling? It's a mix of things.

Competency

The more knowledge you have about the product, the more comfortable you feel in your field. The better your selling skills the easier and almost certainly more enjoyable you'll find your job. The effect of skills (efficacy) on sales performance has been discussed in some detail in Chapter 5.

Clarity

First of all it's vital to have clarity about what your customer wants. In most cases, it's not always so straightforward. Most companies and most deals have more than one stakeholder, so it pays to understand what all of the stakeholders want and not just rely on one opinion.

Driving Sales Results

You also need to have clarity about your own offering, as most companies have a sliding scale of products, pricing and service levels. And you need to have clarity about the value you and your company can bring to the customer. You'll not always have all of the answers when you work on a deal, but the more uncertain you are, the less convincing you're likely to be.

The freedom to walk away from a deal

We've all seen a desperate sales professional. Most sales professionals, at some point in their career, have been desperate. You can only walk away from a deal when you have alternatives. In other words, when you're not relying on one deal to make or break your target. That's why it's so important to have a constant inflow of leads and a healthy pipeline. Desperate deals are normally bad deals. It means you agree to something which you really shouldn't. Having made that point I'm also conscious that nobody is perfect and whilst you should strive to have competence, clarity and the guts to walk away from any deal, the world isn't black and white. What is important to remember is this: optimists sell. So dust yourself off and give it your best shot. Never lose your swagger.

Getting started

Where do you start to get more sales? One of the challenges in discussing the entire subject of sales is that there is no one type of sale. Sales come in many shapes and sizes and your approach has to be tailored accordingly. In this book, I've focused on sales that is relevant for individual sellers (freelancers, consultants) and small companies (start-ups, agencies). Here is a summary and checklist of what we've covered.

1. Are you clear about who your target customer is?
   [Sales Method]
   If not, go back to chapter 2 and revisit some of the ideas there. For some sales professionals, target-customer segments are evolving and the answer might not always be straightforward and simple. In this case, a test-and-learn approach (i.e. trialling different segments) is fine as long as it brings you closer to an answer.

2. Are you clear about your targets?
   [Sales Method]
   What do you need to do to achieve your goals? In this quarter and in the next 12 months? If you don't have a sales process with targets for leads and deals, then revisit chapters 2, 3 and 4. Make a written commitment. Formalising your goals will make all the difference.

3. Do you have a leads list — long enough to take you at least through the next few 4 — 5 weeks?
[Sales Method]
Having leads is fundamental to sales. Ideally, you have a constant stream of warm inbound leads, but the sales world doesn't always work this way. In any case, work on leads should never stop. It's the basis of a healthy pipeline.

4. Do you have your tools in order?
[Sales Method]
If you work towards a plan, you need a system to record your activities. Spreadsheets can only be a temporary solution as CRMs are used for a reason by the overwhelming number of sales professionals. What about the rest of your 'sales stack'? LinkedIn, Sidekick, etc.? Choose and test the tools that you feel are most helpful to your daily sales work.

5. How often do you review your performance?
[Sales Method]
'What gets measured gets managed' as Peter Drucker famously said. If you're working in a team I recommend weekly pipeline reviews. If you're working alone set some time aside once a week and asses the actual performance against plan.

6. Are you learning?
[Sales Skills]
Learning is a journey rather than a destination. In chapter 6 I've outlined skills relevant to sales professionals. That said, there are many more learning exercises that help you to become a better sales professional so don't restrict yourself to the selection outlined in chapter 6.

7. What do you do to keep your sales spirits high?
[Attitude]
Keeping fit is important in every profession, but especially in sales, where some days can be an emotional rollercoast-

er. I found that sports (running) helps me to let steam off, but it might be something different for you. If you haven't found what helps you to be ready for 'showtime', keep looking.

The quickest way to drive more sales is to work on method as you can see from the checklist above.

One of the important messages of the method section is to never stop prospecting. If you don't already process new leads on a regular basis, get started, no matter how low the number. It's better to start with a few leads a month rather than contacting no leads at all. Stick with it, even if you find it hard at the beginning. Hopefully you'll see some early results, but if not, don't despair; some contacts need to be incubated, meaning they might not come through immediately but they will come through down the road. At some point you'll see leads progress into opportunities and older contacts return to resume a previous discussion.

If you have an established sales process, refine it. Set some time aside to analyse your pipeline on a regular basis. Use your insights to improve and iterate your process. For example, increase your inbound lead volume by establishing partnerships where both companies send each other referral contacts.

Be realistic with the opportunities in your pipeline. Don't keep any opportunities in the pipeline out of vanity or laziness. In other words no matter how prominent the company, how big the deal, how nice the contact, if there's no progress you have to remove it from the pipeline. Revisit it at a later stage. Regular pipeline health checks followed by a bi-monthly spring-clean will do the trick.

Regardless of how experienced you are in sales, there's always room for improvement. You can sharpen your skills by engaging in self-directed learning — reading literature, for example, about sales, negotiation, communication or presentation skills. A more practical angle is to record your calls or film yourself during presentation rehearsals. Simplistic, yes, but very useful.

Having a good coach can make working on *attitude* all the easier, but you can do it by yourself as long as you take the time to become self-aware. Check-in with yourself on how you feel before you make a phone call or walk into a meeting. Remember that optimists outsell their peers. Not blind optimism but having an optimistic attitude — approaching the next contact on your list, for instance, with the attitude that he may very well be interested in buying from you as opposed to feeling 'here's another one that will hang up on me'. Those with an optimistic attitude take the approach that deals can be closed despite challenges. They have a 'problem-solver' attitude instead of a 'problem-seeker' mindset.

When I think about sales, I'm sometimes reminded about cooking. I learned a few cooking skills back in high school and even worked in a professional kitchen for a few months. No professional kitchen functions without having a regular supply of groceries and every day there's significant prep work to be done. Peeling potatoes, making sauces, etc. — not the most exciting of work.

When it comes to cooking a dish it's largely down to the proficiency of the cook. Experienced cooks will go freestyle and just cook a recipe by heart. They have the experience, they have cooked it many times before, and know how it should look and taste when it's finished. I have, however, also seen experienced cooks follow a recipe in minute detail when they either haven't previously cooked a particular dish or not done it in a while. They might even go back to a written recipe if they're doing a dish frequently just to make sure they're still in line with the original. A few iterations every week can alter a recipe significantly and the end result might be quite different to the original.

What's this go to do with sales? The prep work is important in both. How you approach an individual sale will depend to a certain extent on your proficiency. The greater your experience, the more freestyle you can go. That said, there's also a danger of being too relaxed about each deal. Checklists have been invented for a reason, because if there are 40 things to consider in the course of a deal, you might be forgiven for not being able to remember all of them. So, it's OK to go freestyle from time to time as sales isn't a static profession. It's as much an art as it is science. But ignoring your 'prep work', your prospecting, is likely to cost you dearly.

Summary

I hope you found this book useful and informative, and that you implement some of the advice found here to drive sales results for your business. Selling is deal-making. Dealmakers are the heroes of our time.

References

Adamsen, Brent, Dixon, Matthew and Toman Nicholas (2013) *Dismantling the Sales Machine*, Harvard Business Review

Ali, Abdul, Onyemah, Vincent and Pesquera, Martha Rivera (2013) *What Entrepreneurs Get Wrong*, Harvard Business Review

Barker, Tansu A. (1999), *Benchmarks of Successful Salesforce Performance*, Canadian Journal of Administrative Sciences

Broughton, Philip Delves (2012), *Life's A Pitch: What the World's Best Sales People Can Teach Us All*, Penguin

Boyer, Stefanie L. and Lambert, Brian (2008), *Take the Handcuffs off Sales Team Development with Self-Directed Learning*, American Society for Training and Development

Cuddy, Amy (2012) *Your body language shapes who you are*, www.ted.com/talks (accessed 20 July 2015)

Christensen, Clayton M., Cook, Scott and Hall, Taddy (2006) *What Customers Want from Your Products*, Harvard Business School

DeCormier, Ray A., Jobber, David (1993), *The Counselor Selling Method: Concepts and Constructs*, Journal of Personal Selling and Sales Management

Dixon, Andrea L., and Susan M.B. Schertzer (2005), *Bouncing Back: How Salesperson Optimism and Self-Efficacy Influence Attributions and Behaviors Following Failure*, Journal of Personal Selling & Sales Management

Felicia G. Lassk, Thomas N. Ingram, Florian Kraus, and Rita Di Mascio (2012), *The Future of Sales Training: Challenges and Related Research Questions*, Journal of Personal Selling and Sales Management

Frayne, Colette A. and Geringer, J. Michael (2000), *Self-Management Training for Improving Job Performance: A Field Experiment Involving Salespeople*, Journal of Applied Psychology

Fu, Frank Q., Richards, Keith A. and Eli Jones (2009), *The Motivation Hub: Effects of Goal Setting and Self-Efficacy on Effort and New Product Sales*, Journal of Personal Selling and Sales Management

Heath, Chip and Heath, Dan (2007), *Made to Stick: Why Some Ideas Survive and Others Die*, Random House

Jobber, David and Lancaster, Geoffrey (2009), *Selling and sales management*, Harlow: Pearson Education Limited

Klaff, Oren (2011), *Pitch Anything: An Innovative method for Presenting, Persuading, and Winning the Deal*, McGraw-Hill

Krishnan, Balaji C., Netemeyer, Richard G. and Boles, James S. Self-Efficacy (2002), *Competitiveness, and Effort as Antecedents of Salesperson Performance*, Journal of Personal Selling and Sales Management

Locke, Edwin A., Latham, Gary P. (2002), *Building a Practically Useful Theory of Goal Setting and Task Motivation*, American Psychologist

Luthans, Fred, Avey, James B., Avolio, Bruce J. and Peterson, Suzanne J. (2010), *The Development and Resulting Performance Impact of Positive Psychological Capital*, Human Resource Development Quarterly

Miao, Fred C. and Evans, Kenneth R. (2007), *The Impact of Salesperson Motivation on Role Perceptions and Job Performance — A Cognitive and Affective Perspective*, Journal of Personal Selling & Sales Management

Morris, Desmond (2002), *Peoplewatching: The Desmond Morris Guide to Body Language*, Random House eBooks

Navarro, Joe and Karlins, Marlin (2007), *What Every Body is Saying*, HarperCollins e-books

Porter, Michael E. (1980), *Competitive Strategy*, New York: Free Press

Pink, Daniel H. (2012), *To Sell is Human: The surprising truth about moving others*, New York: Riverhead Books

Seligman, Martin E.P. (1990), *Learned Optimism: How to Change Your Mind and Your Life*, Random House

Sullivan, Tim (2000), *Evaluating Sales Training Programs: Determining the Effectiveness of Sales Training Programs*, Siebel Systems White Paper, San Mateo, CA

Turner, Josh (2015), *Connect: The Secret LinkedIn Playbook To Generate Leads, Build Relationships, And Dramatically Increase Your Sales*, Lioncrest Publishing

William L. Cron, Greg W. Marshall, Jagdip Singh, Rosann L. Spiro, and Harish Sujan (2005), *Salesperson Selection, Training and Development: Trends, Implications and Research Opportunities*, Journal of Personal Selling and Sales Management

About the Author

Wolf Depauli has worked in sales for many years. From selling consumer goods to software solutions, from closing partnership deals to building new business propositions from scratch. He's been a top seller in teams of up to 15 sales professionals working for top brands in the world of sales. Experienced in handling all aspects of sales from defining the proposition, generating leads, managing the pipeline and closing deals, Wolf has a deep insight about the challenges sales professionals face and what you can do to ensure you succeed.

Wolf grew up in Austria before moving to London where he now lives with his wife.

Printed in Great Britain
by Amazon